# Prologue

I was born Marie and I will die Lulu. This book is about the journey between those two people, losing parts of myself, finding others and all the many shapes I've bent myself into over sixty years in the music business. Because I've always tried to be honest, but haven't been completely open. The reason? I grew up in a home filled with secrets before being catapulted into fame at just fifteen with no idea of who I even was. And so, I became whoever I thought people wanted me to be.

Bright, bubbly, always smiling.

That face who's been on your TV and radio for years.

It's who I am in some ways, of course. I'm definitely positive. And I've certainly been around for decades. But the image of me created when I was young was as one-dimensional as a single ray of light is compared to its infinite refractions. Still a child in so many ways, I took on the part created for me and played it so well, I gradually lost who I was; I became the version of myself I thought people wanted me to be. Not just in public, but personally too. And I paid a price for moulding myself into so many shapes and forms until life, as it often does, forced me to take a long, hard look and finally answer the question, 'Who am I?'

It has taken time to unravel and dismantle all the many layers I've hidden beneath to protect myself from a young age and avoid hard truths. But I finally have. I know who I am. And now I'm ready to tell the whole story, instead of just parts of it: from the highs of joy, success and love, to the lows of addiction, divorce and failure – plus all the colours in between.

Most of all, this is the story of being a fallible, imperfect human. A woman. I hope parts of it resonate.

It's finally time to be completely transparent.

So here we go.

This book is dedicated to my family.
My son Jordan
My daughter-in-law Alanna
My grandchildren Bella & Teddy
My brother Billy
My sister Edwina
My brother Gordon

# If Only You Knew

# If Only You Knew

*Lulu*

**HODDER &
STOUGHTON**

First published in Great Britain in 2025 by Hodder & Stoughton Limited
An Hachette UK company

The authorised representative in the EEA is Hachette Ireland, 8 Castlecourt
Centre, Dublin 15, D15 XTP3, Ireland (email: info@hbgi.ie)

1

'Poison Kiss' (p. 305)
Written by Cregan/Kennedy/Lawrie
Published by Fairwood Music (UK) Ltd
Used with permission. All Rights Reserved.

'Every Single Day' (p. 305–306)
Written by Kennedy/Lawrie/Weaver
Published by Fairwood Music (UK) Ltd/Kassner Associated Publishers Ltd
Used with permission. All Rights Reserved.

A CIP catalogue record for this title is available from the British Library

Hardback ISBN 9781399744249
Trade Paperback ISBN 9781399744256
ebook ISBN 9781399744263

Typeset in Electra by Hewer Text UK Ltd
Printed and bound in Great Britain by Clays Ltd, Elcograf S.p.A.

Hodder & Stoughton policy is to use papers that are natural, renewable
and recyclable products and made from wood grown in sustainable
forests. The logging and manufacturing processes are expected to
conform to the environmental regulations of the country of origin.

Hodder & Stoughton Limited
Carmelite House
50 Victoria Embankment
London EC4Y 0DZ

www.hodder.co.uk

# Contents

## III

## IV

## V

# Contents

I

# 1

# All I Want to Do Is Sing

I was glad I'd borrowed Mum's leather jacket. Otherwise, I might have shivered and I didn't want to look scared. In front of me, a row of men sat behind a huge sound desk, cigarette smoke curling into the air as they chatted.

'Ready to go?' a voice asked.

It was summer 1963 and the Gleneagles boys were standing with me in a Decca studio: Jimmy, on rhythm guitar; Ross, the lead guitarist; Dave our drummer; bassist Tommy; and Alex, also a vocalist. We'd been performing together for a couple of years in clubs, but never anywhere like this. There have been so many people, places and performances since then, but, even though I was just fourteen, I'd already been performing my whole life.

We'd been brought to London after winning a competition in the *Scottish Daily Express* to find the next big thing. The prize was an audition with Ron Richards, a producer at EMI, home of the Beatles. But although he'd turned us down, he'd sent us on to see Dick Rowe at Decca. The Rolling Stones were signed there so it didn't feel like too much of a knock back. Now, as I stood waiting, I forced myself to shrink once more into that safe place deep inside me where only my voice mattered. I wasn't quite sure what I was supposed to do. Who I was supposed to be. But I knew how to sing. Pulling down the mic, I glanced at the Gleneagles boys for a final time before staring ahead.

'Ready Marie?' a voice asked.

I nodded and took a deep breath. We'd done this track hundreds of times before. I just had to relax and hit the first notes right. That was the key. Breathing deeply, I looked up and let the first long, vibrating, almost angry note pour out of me, the sound cascading into the mic. Powerful. Raw.

A man behind the desk raised his hand.

'Hold a minute, there's something wrong with the mic,' he said as I stopped singing.

He was a young engineer called Gus Dudgeon who would go on to produce some of Elton John's biggest work. But, that day, none of us had any clue what the future held for us.

'Oh my God,' Gus said as he walked up to check the microphone. 'She's blown the ribbon.'

The Decca men looked at each other and started laughing. Tiny girl. Big voice. I got that a lot. Then an elegant man in a slim-fitting navy suit and tie, a producer called Peter Sullivan, leaned forwards.

'Why not take a step back Marie?' he said. 'We'll do it again. Go from the top.'

So I did what Peter asked: nodded and moved back from the mic – obedient and pliable as always. Ready to perform and give whatever my audience wanted from me. And I'd keep on doing it for decades to come.

I took a deep breath and started to sing again.

# 2

# I Just Want to Fit In

'Go check your daddy is sleeping,' my mother, Betty, whispered as she bent down to take out the half bottle of whisky my father kept stashed under the sink.

Throughout my childhood, Betty would sneak out the bottles to water them down, but I was never quite sure why. A splash of water wasn't going to make much of a difference. Dad had been in bed since he got in from the pub. Just like most days.

It was about two months after the Decca audition and, while the Gleneagles and I had been signed within a few days, nothing much had happened since then. Decca had wanted to sign just me at first, but I'd refused. I didn't want to do this alone. I'd always been in a band. I liked performing with people. I couldn't just drop my friends.

Sensing my resistance, Decca had agreed to sign us all, but we now had to wait until I turned fifteen in November 1963 because I couldn't legally leave school until then and needed to go on the road to promote a single. I had no idea what they even meant by 'promotion', and neither did my parents, but none of us dared ask questions, and the waiting back home in Glasgow felt one part intolerable, another surreal. Marie McDonald

McLaughlin Lawrie had been signed to a record label. The neighbours were agog.

Betty, however, was less convinced.

'You're so young,' she said now as she took the cork out of the bottle and dribbled cold water into it. 'I just don't think this is right. A girl on her own in London. Who knows what happens there?'

'But I won't be alone!' I cried. 'I'll be with the band. And I'm not leaving home Mammy.'

Betty sighed.

'I don't understand why hairdressing isn't good enough for you Marie. Why can't you just sing on weekends like you always have?'

I looked at my mother, anxious to convince her. Girls like me didn't get to do things like this. I understood that. All any parent where I came from aspired to was for their sons to move up in the world by becoming a boxer or a footballer, while girls were expected to grow up, work in a factory or as a hairdresser, get married and look after children. Just as our mothers and grandmothers before us had done.

'Let's just see what happens Mammy,' I pleaded. 'I have to give it a try.'

I looked at my mother, silently willing her to agree as she stared back at me, eyes narrowed in thought.

'Okay,' Betty said at last before tucking the bottle back under the sink.

No more was said as I scurried back to my bedroom. But the weeks dragged by as I waited for my birthday and spent a lot of time staring at the Beatles posters covering my walls, no idea where it was all headed. I was thrilled I had a record coming out, but no sense of what that might mean. And most of the bands I knew were made up of twenty-something men: the Animals, the Kinks, Gerry and the Pacemakers. A new one called the Rolling Stones was also emerging. And a female singer, too, called Dusty Springfield who I loved. She had just gone solo after years of success with the Springfields.

Where on earth would Marie Lawrie fit into all that?

# 3

# No Pushover

Growing up in Fifties Glasgow meant you hardly saw a blade of grass and certainly no cows or sheep. And even though it was a big city, I lived largely within the confines of just a few concrete streets in the East End of Glasgow. The area was called the Gallowgate and it was packed with families living cheek by jowl in tenement blocks. Poverty and violence were common, and so was trouble between local Protestant and Catholic gangs.

The first home I lived in on Soho Street had two rooms: one, where we cooked and ate, had a coal fireplace, two armchairs and a fold-up bed for my parents; the other was stuffed with a wardrobe, dressing table, three-piece suite and another fold-up bed for me and my brother Billy. There was no bathroom, toilet or separate kitchen. Instead, we'd strip wash at a sink next to the cooker in a tiny scullery and shower once a week in the mobile units the Glasgow Corporation brought into the school playground. Privacy was a luxury no one could afford.

But while my childhood has often been described as 'poor', I hate that word. Poor doesn't encapsulate a world which was so rich in community, love and the tight bonds between close-knit working-class families. And, financially, my family was also far better off than many. By the time I was about eight, for instance, we'd left Soho Street for a new tenement on Garfield Street, which was only a few minutes away, but officially in Dennistoun, a cut above the Gallowgate. One of eight flats in a small block, our new home had two bedrooms, its own toilet and a living room with a kitchenette off it. Like all tenement flats, it also had large alcoves built into the walls to be used as sleeping spaces – vital given that my sister Edwina was born when I was ten, and baby Gordon arrived two years after that. Six of us were packed into the two-bedroom flat which was permanently busy, noisy and chaotic.

The reason we could afford to move was because my father, Eddie, was … an entrepreneur? A thief? I'm not quite sure. Not that Eddie considered himself a criminal, of course. Neither did anyone else. Glasgow was the kind of place where you took your chances, and you were a fool to ignore one if it presented itself – which my father's job at the meat market did. I hated the place. The unusual smell and freezing cold. But I learned to hide my fear whenever Dad took me there as a child, knowing I had to be brave because he was letting me into his world.

Eddie worked at the market as an offal dresser and was up before dawn each day for a 5am shift in the huge hanger of a building where he spent the next few hours gutting animal carcasses strung up on pulleys above his head. Arriving home with trousers stiff with dried blood and smelling of disinfectant, he'd plunge them into a bucket to soak before getting changed. Occasionally, he'd also have to see to a cut on his hand if his knife had slipped. However bad it was though, however deep, Eddie never saw a doctor to get stitches for fear they'd restrict his movement and ability to work. Instead, he'd stick a lump of Vaseline onto the wound before wrapping it in gauze.

'Got to be able to work,' my dad would say proudly as he looked at his scarred hands. 'Never missed a day in my life.'

Eddie was a hard worker. No doubt about it. But there was another important reason why he was so dedicated: the opportunity the meat market gave him to create a second income selling on whatever he'd managed to snaffle. Local butchers loved Eddie Lawrie for the abundant supply of liver, tripe and other offal he could get his hands on. Some of it was swapped for extras that other families couldn't afford, like fresh fish, but mostly it was sold on to bring in a precious second income to our home.

My parents, however, had to be careful to hide the extra cash which my mother often stuffed at the back of drawers and under the lino. Because back then, Glasgow was the kind of place where you were cut down to size if your head went too far above the rest, and Betty and Eddie had made some mistakes early on with too many new clothes, coats and shoes. One neighbour was so incensed by the Lawries parading around in their finery, they'd paid a thug to attack my father. Thirty shillings, apparently, was all it took to persuade someone to slice Eddie's face with a razor. Like I said, no one where I came from passed up an opportunity to make extra money.

I never knew if my father got his own back, but I'm sure he must have waited, watched and attacked back when he got the chance. He had no other choice because you could never, ever show weakness in Glasgow. If you did, you'd be walked over. Where I came from, standing your ground wasn't a weakness; it was a strength.

# 4

# You're a Lulu of a Kid

After finally turning fifteen, I went back to London to prepare for the official release of 'Shout'. Marian Massey was
now managing me and the Gleneagles because her brother
Tony was one of the people who'd got us down to London as the
rise of British music, kicked off by Beatlemania, sparked a talent
gold rush. And although Marian hadn't worked in music before,
she came from a family of businessmen and was ambitious.
Everyone seemed sure she'd be able to do the job, including my
parents.

'I think a woman will be better looking after a wee lassie,'
Eddie had declared.

I'd been hoping to record something other than 'Shout' for
our first release. The band and I had been doing it in local clubs
for a while, but Decca felt the way we performed it sounded new
and fresh, so we'd recorded it a few weeks before with our producer Peter Sullivan.

As I stood in the studio late in the day, Marian had swept in
wearing a Persian lamb coat with a huge chinchilla collar over
a black pencil skirt, round neck sweater (probably cashmere),
accessorised with pearls, big gold earrings (probably Chanel)

and a bright red lip. I, meanwhile, had a heavy cold and my hair was in rollers because I was hoping to be taken out for a pizza or something that night.

Marian had taken one look at me, turned to Peter Sullivan and spoken to him in her commanding voice.

'Look at her!' she exclaimed as I blew my nose. 'This child shouldn't be working when she's clearly so unwell.'

I stared at Marian wordlessly. No one ever asked whether I should be on stage or not. Cold or no cold. I'd always turned up, however I was feeling.

'I think we've done enough here today,' she declared, her tone commanding, certain.

Then she put her arm around me.

'Let's go and get you something for that cold,' she said and whisked me out of the studio leaving the Gleneagles boys to pack up and Peter fuming.

I soon sank into one of the leather seats in Marian's car as she plunged into the busy London traffic like a gladiator going into the ring. Marian, I started to learn that day, did everything decisively. Hitting the accelerator, slamming the brakes, snaking in and out of traffic, she drove me to Marylebone where we pulled up in front of a huge, wooden-fronted shop. As we walked inside, the warm air was filled with a mixture of perfume, cough medicine and something almost antiseptic trailing underneath it all. Assistants in white coats rushed up to us, pulling out pills and potions that Marian bought with a crisp £1 note before popping them into her crocodile bag and snapping it shut.

'John Bell & Croyden is the best pharmacy in town,' she said as she strode away from the counter. 'Now, let's get you tucked up in bed and I'm sure you'll feel far better in the morning.'

Amid all the new faces in the swirl of activity as we started preparing to release 'Shout', Marian felt like a creature from an entirely different planet. A trained opera singer, she spoke with a clipped English voice and was married to a wealthy business-man called Gerald Massey. But even though they had three school-age children, and Marian could easily have spent her life having lunch and doing her hair, she wanted to do more.

Marian's house in Holland Park had loomed above me when I'd arrived to see her a couple of weeks after recording 'Shout'. Her housekeeper had opened the door, formally dressed for domestic duties, and shown me into the largest front room I'd ever seen in my life. The walls were drenched in art (including a huge portrait of Marian looking regal), there were plump sofas, a grand piano, shelves covered in china, and trays groaning under twinkling glass. It was the kind of house I'd only ever seen flickering on a big screen when I went to the Geggie, Scotia or Orient with my mum. I might as well have been on Mars.

Then Marian arrived. She was the most glamorous thing I'd ever seen. With amazing shiny hair. So luxurious. Mine was so full of hairspray, I'd go up in flames if anyone got too close with a match, I thought to myself.

'Your name, Marie, we've got to change it,' Marian said as she – and her hair – paced up and down the thick carpet that cov-ered her sitting room floor and I sat at a piano beside Tony.

'What makes you different is your energy. Your confidence. You're like a breath of fresh air. But we need a name that sums all that up.'

Marian and Tony had been throwing around ideas for a while now without much success: 'Too boring'. 'We need something that really describes her.'

'Roxy?' Tony asked.

'God no!' Marian exclaimed. 'Makes her sound like a go-go dancer.'

And then came the moment when Marian, who as well as living in a spaceship-sized house had also spent a lot of time in America, which, as far as I was concerned, was the promised land, turned and threw her hands up in the air.

'Well, all I know is that she's a real lulu of a kid.'

I had no idea what 'lulu' meant, but Tony and Marian looked at each other as if they'd just cracked the code for nuclear fusion.

'That's it,' said Tony. 'Lulu. Perfect. It's great.'

Later, I learned that the definition of 'lulu' is *'remarkable'* and, in time, I realised that the reason Marian saw me this way was because I'd been dialling up parts of myself and damping down others for years before she met me, hiding so many feelings and becoming whoever I needed to be as a performer. She, like many others, saw me as gutsy. Confident. Bright. And I was. Or at least that's how I'd learned to present myself to the world.

And so that was the day I started to become a new person. No longer just plain old Marie, the 'wee belter' from Glasgow. I was now Lulu, and I'd learn to inhabit her so well, I'd be fixed there for decades to come.

Youthful.
Perky.
Always smiling.
Whatever people wanted of me.

# 5

# Finding My Voice

I've never been one of those people who glide quietly through life, the kind who speak softly, rarely raise their voice or get too incensed about anything. Neither was anyone in my family. The Lawries were loud. Emotional. Passionate. And I knew from before I could remember what I was most passionate about: singing. My voice was always a mismatch with my size though. It was always bigger than me, which is why it got me noticed even when I was young.

Picture the scene: eight-year-old, four-foot-nothing me, lifted onto a chair to reach a microphone in front of a big Blackpool holiday crowd. It felt like I'd been singing ever since I was born, to friends and neighbours, entering competitions and obsessed with music. Now, I was standing in front of a sea of holidaymakers, dressed in pristine white sandals with matching bobby socks and a sticky out frock with a bow on the back. I stared up at the talent show compère as the chair beneath me rocked unsteadily.

'Careful little girl,' he said.

I stared up at him defiantly. I'll show you.

The audience readied themselves for a rendition of 'Baa Baa Black Sheep'. Instead, I launched into 'The Garden of Eden' – a

Joe Valino hit which had been covered in the UK by Frankie Vaughan – in a voice that was one part child, another blues singer who's seen the harder parts of life and was recounting it all over a bottle of bourbon and twenty Marlboros. This was the kind of singing I'd listened to and, lucky for me, my voice came out sounding similar.

Aged nine, I got my first paid gig performing songs during the intervals of the Caledonian Marching Band's Sunday concerts. Standing on stage, singing in front of hundreds of people, I'd experienced the power of connection to an audience for the very first time. It felt like coming home. Soon after starting secondary school, I'd graduated to fronting local bands – the Bellrocks and then the Gleneagles. Playing at Glasgow clubs and US airbases, I'd sing American music like Inez and Charlie Foxx's 'Mockingbird' and Brenda Lee's 'Let's Jump the Broomstick'.

My dad was the one with music in his soul. And his voice was the essence of who he was: emotional, powerful at times, gentle at others. Eddie Lawrie was a small, handsome man, with shoes he polished so bright you could see your face in them, and the man who gave me the gift of song. But most people we knew were great singers, lots of them better than me, because Glasgow then was a city filled with music. In pubs and living rooms, concert halls and churches, people gathered together to either sing or listen to others. No one where I came from sat down with a glass of wine to discuss politics or feelings. Music was the glue that drew us together, created a sense of community and softened the hard edges of difficult lives.

Weekends were the highlight: a wage packet earned and enough money to buy a couple of drinks. Most Fridays, our flat would fill with friends like Alec Crichton, a handsome Merchant Navy seaman, and his mother Big May, who was always dressed in a shirt and tie for her job as a chauffeur to a city bigwig. Alec had the kind of good, thick hair my mother adored. Paranoid about her own, Betty was constantly changing its colour and never held back expressing her bitter disappointment that I'd ended up with 'two hairs and a shugly' instead of thick Shirley Temple curls.

Jimmy Graham, an old navy friend of my father's, might also drop in with his wife May, or James Goldie with his ma Emmie, who worked as an office cleaner. And often, my father's cousin, wee Auntie Netty, would be wedged in too, along with a couple of neighbours.

As cigarette smoke hung thick as pork chops in the air, the men – and Big May – would pour a whisky with a dash of water while the women sat with a vodka and orange, sherry or Advocaat and lemonade.

'Gi'e us a song Eddie,' someone would eventually say because my father loved crooners like Perry Como, Frank Sinatra, Nat King Cole or Mario Lanza and would sing them in his rich, deep voice.

Most nights too, someone would also eventually ask after me.

'Can you get wee Marie up? Let's get her tae sing.'

'No,' Betty would answer. 'Let her sleep.'

But, more often than not, I'd wake up, hear my father singing and creep out of bed before peeping around the door.

'Can ah sing?' I'd ask, and my father would come and pick me up.

'Go on darlin',' he'd say. 'Give us your best.'

And even though I was young, I could sing pretty much anything from Connie Francis' 'Lipstick on Your Collar' to Caterina Valente's Spanish folk song 'La Malagueña', which was a bit left of centre and hard to sing. My dad loved that I could do it and my grandfather would cry when he heard me.

'Where did she get that voice?' people would murmur as they listened. 'She's got an old soul that one.'

'Voice like a coalman,' Eddie would proudly reply.

Those nights singing for my parents and their friends are some of my happiest childhood memories. Because even though I was so young, I was lucky enough to recognise something deep inside which allowed me to communicate with people in a unique way.

# 6

# Beatlemania

Friday nights were about two things in the Lawrie home: a fish and chip supper and the TV. My parents had gone out and left me to put Edwina, who was five, and three-year-old Gordon to bed. Billy was at the chippie and I was waiting for *Around the Beatles* to start on TV. The boys had filmed a special and, like the rest of the UK – and now America – I was hanging out to see it.

Three weeks previously, 'Shout' had been released and I'd gone back down to London to perform on *Ready Steady Go!* – the biggest pop TV show of the moment. Even just a few years before, there had been nothing like it on TV, but the revolution in music meant everything was moving at lightning speed and teenagers now wanted their own television, music and clothes.

'You're going to be brilliant,' Marian had said as we waited backstage for me to perform. 'Just do what you always do.'

Marian, I was discovering, seemed to think I was capable of anything. She kept talking about all the other things I'd be able to do, but I really didn't have a clue what she was talking about. I was a singer. That was what I did. What I wanted to do.

'Oh Lu,' Marian said with a laugh when I told her. 'Look at how young you are and how quickly you pick things up. You're fearless, you always go for it. I want everyone to see your talent.'

It's amazing how fast you can adapt, particularly when you're young and unformed. And I was a teenage girl too, so the only thing that I kept thinking about before appearing on TV was what on earth I'd wear. I'd grown up with Betty worrying constantly about her hair, the size of her nose and her weight. She spent hours trawling markets and expensive shops looking for bargains in her constant pursuit of trying to make herself feel better by looking just right. And Betty's preoccupation with how you must present yourself to the world had snaked its way inside me.

In the end, Marian and I decided on a striped T-shirt, some clamdiggers and a pair of flat shoes. I didn't have a wardrobe full of clothes to wear, and Marian kept telling me that young girls should be able to see themselves in me. Miming to 'Shout', I walked down a spiral staircase and onto a dance floor crowded with teenagers while the Gleneagles – who'd also been renamed and were now known as the Luvvers – played. When the track ended, the host Michael Aldred interviewed me and I tried to slow down my voice and round out the sound because most people in London couldn't seem to understand a word I said. It embarrassed me almost as much as realising that my gold tooth, the legacy of many Glaswegian children with limited access to dentistry, risked looking like a gaping hole at the wrong angle on a black and white TV picture. Marian had told me we'd need to get it fixed.

After the show finished and we were getting ready to leave, one of the producers came up to me and Marian:

'We're going to San Lorenzo,' she said. 'Would you like to join us?'

I soon discovered that San Lorenzo was an Italian restaurant when we arrived to find it packed with people, noise and Bobby Darin sitting on a corner table. I'd always adored him. Bobby was adaptable; he could sing in so many styles and infused his music with soul. I couldn't eat a bite of my food as people chatted around the table and I kept sneaking looks at him. But then, as he got up to leave, Bobby walked towards our table.

'Hey Lulu,' he said as he stopped beside me.

Marian and the *Ready Steady Go!* crew stared at me expectantly.

'Hello,' I finally stammered.

'I saw you on TV tonight,' Bobby drawled. 'You were great. Good luck with everything.'

And then he was gone. I ran out to a payphone, scrabbled around in my purse for enough change to feed into it and screamed at Betty the moment she picked up.

'Mammy! It's me! I'm in a restaurant with Marian. And I've just met Bobby Darrin!'

I'm pretty sure the whole of Dennistoun heard Betty when she screamed back at me. But now, just a few days later, I was back at home again, back to being Marie. It felt like going back to black and white after being plunged into technicolour.

The clock hands slid on until *Around the Beatles* finally started and I watched as Ringo appeared wearing a medieval doublet, and a crowd of banner-waving teenagers poured into a theatre. The boys seemed to be doing Shakespeare, but I'd never read a word of it so couldn't be sure. The show continued. Cilla Black sang 'You're My World' and Millie Small did 'My Boy Lollipop'. And then, at last, the boys came on to perform. 'Twist and Shout' was followed by a succession of hits culminating in 'I Want to Hold Your Hand'. I walked over to the TV to sit even closer, staring at Paul intently, as obsessed as every other teenage girl by him. And his perfect hair.

'Thank you, thank you very much, and God bless you,' John said to the screaming crowd as the show drew to a close. 'You've got a lucky face. The end.'

And then a miracle happened. Or at least it felt like one to me. The studio went silent before George hit an F major chord and the camera panned to Paul.

'You know you make me wanna shout,' he wailed.

The crowd screamed, the boys launched into the single I'd just released and I almost peed my pants in excitement. Eight days later, 'Shout' entered the charts at number forty-one and started climbing steadily. I've always been convinced that I have the Beatles to thank for launching me. Who knows what might have happened if they hadn't done 'Shout' that day? By the middle of June, the single had reached number seven. But, by then, I was so busy I hardly noticed because everything had exploded.

# 7

# Fifteen Years Old and on My Way

Stoke, Great Yarmouth and Corby, Harrogate, Manchester and Wisbech. Those first few months after 'Shout' became a hit are mostly a blur. It felt as if me, the Luvvers and Marian were permanently packed into the battered old van we used for travelling, bursting out of it to set up, perform and maybe do an interview for a local newspaper, TV station or national music magazine, before getting back in again to head to the next stop.

There were two reasons why we didn't stop: Marian wanted us to make the most of being in the charts and we hadn't got an advance from Decca so needed to earn money. With a hit record, our fee had gone up to £100, which seemed like a huge amount – even when we split it – because I'd only just left school and the Luvvers boys had been working as electricians, joiners or window cleaners until now.

Marian was rapidly proving herself an inspired choice to manage us. Undaunted by our new world, we were quickly building a team around us that included our new agent Dick Katz and a PR man called Leslie Perrin, a journalist turned publicist with a face like a Pekingese dog, who was known for building careers overnight and diffusing scandals even more quickly.

He famously went on to represent the Rolling Stones who, I presume, didn't need his career-building skills.

Together, they got us on all the local radio and TV stations and we also performed solo, as well as on bills alongside acts like the Applejacks, Millie Small and Gene Vincent. My name was in and out of the press too and, within a couple of months, I'd topped the *Record Mirror*'s poll for 'Most Promising Young Singer'.

'Shout' was a huge hit and interest in Lulu – the new 'teen sensation' – was high. I wasn't the first schoolgirl singer. Helen Shapiro had been there before and we were similar in some ways because her voice was also deep. But mine had a rawer edge and there was a difference in our energy. I was out there, up front and working the stage. In fact, I was heading up an all-male band with a swagger, and that made me different. This was what had made Decca see my potential and, just as they'd predicted, teens related to me.

I was working harder than ever, and the feeling which rushed up in me now as I walked onto a stage and saw a huge crowd was electrifying. Pure energy filled me as I sang to bigger and bigger audiences. It was like a drug. And the larger the crowds got, the more powerful the connection I felt. It was unlike anything I'd ever known. And I couldn't get enough of it.

Surreal. Euphoric even.

I was just beginning to feel my power.

But if performing felt like flying, getting into bed in a B&B in somewhere like Wigan felt like crashing back down to earth. Loneliness would fill me – missing home, my family, everything that was familiar to me. The rooms felt so quiet, even with Marian in the room next door. I was used to a home packed with people, noise, motion and chaos. I loved looking after the little ones, and I missed Billy and my parents too. Now, suddenly, here I was, lying in my own bed, no small child sleeping next to me – just this deep, impenetrable silence that left me feeling like I was floating in deep space alone. I'd never had the chance to feel lonely before. But in those lonely, dark hours late at night, my mind would start whirring and my anxiety would kick in. Fear grows in the dark. Every little worry gets bigger until morning light reveals the solutions. Night after night, I'd cry myself to sleep, feeling almost guilty. I was living every teenage girl's dream. So what was I worried about?

When you're fifteen and full of emotions that push and pull, you can't take a step back and just accept it's part of the process. I was ashamed of feeling in any way unhappy, of letting anything puncture the exhilaration of having a hit record and gratitude for the stroke of luck, or fate, that had somehow pushed me into the spotlight.

One thing sustained me, though: camaraderie with the Luvvers and everyone else who was on the road with us. Wherever we went, all roads seemed to lead back to the M1 – and we'd walk into the Blue Boar services late at night to find anyone from the Animals to the Kinks sitting with a full English. It wasn't just me who was part of this new scene. British music was exploding and new acts were coming up all over.

The High Numbers for instance, who became the Who, got the red-carpet treatment when they came back to my parents' after we all did a gig at Kelvin Hall in Glasgow. To celebrate, my dad got out the bottle of Chivas he kept at the back of the sideboard ready for special occasions, and Keith Moon had stared at me with his lovely puppy dog eyes which also felt terrifyingly intense to a fifteen-year-old. It was probably the amphetamines.

Musicians who'd go on to become huge stars were working as session musicians and I recorded with many of them when we went back into the studio to start working on new material. Highly trained and efficient, the session guys were the musical equivalent of Bolshoi ballet performers: disciplined and ruthless at execution. Jimmy Page was one and turned up to a recording session with his guitar and a thing he called a 'fuzz box'. It sounded like a baby blowing a raspberry to me. He'd go on to change musical history with it.

A few months in, I also heard an incredible voice when I went in to do a vocal for Peter Sullivan and he was playing 'It's Not Unusual'.

'Who's that?' I asked.

'A guy I've just signed called Tom Jones.'

Ironically for someone called Lulu, I thought it was a stupid name. *Tom Jones* was a film. Not a pop star. People would get confused. Wrong on that one too. And a certain Reginald Dwight was also knocking about by then.

# 8

# That's What They Do in London

'I'll have the escargots,' Marian's handsome American brother-in-law said.

'Dripping in garlic,' someone else exclaimed, and the women at the table heaved a collective sigh of appreciation.

We were having dinner at the White Elephant on Curzon Street in Mayfair and I watched as a waiter poured chilled white wine into glasses. I knew I wouldn't be able to drink it. Too sharp. I preferred the sweetness of Mateus Rosé. Staring down at the cutlery in front of me, I wondered what on earth I should do with it all as the waiter started taking the women's orders.

'I'll have escargots too please,' I said in a rush when it was my turn because I'd quickly learned three things: stay quiet, smile and copy what everyone else did.

Relief flooded though me when the food finally arrived and I realised that escargots were just posh whelks. The kind we got back home from the local market and sucked out of their shells. Now, though, I had a strange little contraption to do that for me.

Right from the start, Marian was far more than a manager. And it wasn't just the clothes and glamour. It was everything about her. I was in the presence of a sophistication I had never seen before and wanted to emulate. Marian and Gerald had a housekeeper and a cook. They holidayed in the south of France. Gerry had gone to Syracuse University in America, which is why they often went there. It was becoming clear to me how small my world had been before and how vast was the one Marian was introducing me to. I couldn't get enough.

Marian had her hair done at Vidal Sassoon. Her nails were short and perfectly painted. Her car had leather seats. My parents didn't even have a car, but the seats would have been plastic if they did. She took me to a high-end dentist called Fison Clarke on Harley Street to finally get my gold tooth replaced with a sparkling white crown.

Marian was cosmopolitan and sophisticated, and I was entranced. She knew what to eat, read and wear, how to decorate a home and talk to anyone. I watched, hungry to learn, trying to blend into my new world, warping myself around the shapes that Marian showed me. More and more, she felt like the safe centre of a universe that was spinning wildly around me and a guide into a life I'd never even known existed.

Marian, for instance, was always putting on her lipstick, and I'd watch in fascination as she did it without a mirror, sweeping a perfect carmine arc across her lips anywhere from at the hairdresser to in a restaurant as if it was the most natural thing in the world.

'What are you doing?' Betty had screeched when she first saw me doing the same.

'That's what they do in London,' I told her.

I was entranced by Marian. But the strangest thing? She seemed as fascinated by me as I was by her.

'You can do anything you set your mind to,' she'd say again and again as she watched me work and work and work, never complaining, never saying I couldn't get out of bed, never saying no.

I was used to it. I'd been performing for a long time and came from a place where people worked every hour to make ends meet. And while I had no idea why Marian was so taken with me, I think I was as alien to her as she was to me, a working-class kid who knuckled down immediately to whatever I was given to do. Plus, I had that 'lulu' spirit. Whatever nerves I felt, whatever fear, I hid it. I smiled, said yes and entertained, aware that I'd been given an opportunity I had to make the most of.

I'd always been a versatile singer, able to flip my voice from a crystal operatic sound to a gritty soul one with ease, but now I started to adapt the rest of myself too. Bit by bit, I softened my accent, flattened it out, sounding more like Marian by the day. As the months passed, I grew my hair out from its chunky bright red bob to a longer, softer style.

My fashion changed as well. While I loved rock and wanted to carry on wearing my mum's black leather jacket, Marian quickly cleaned me up, presenting me to the world as a wholesome, clean-cut teenager.

'No, not that darling,' she said when we visited her husband's wholesale clothing business to rifle through the racks. 'How about these?'

Holding up a tasteful shift dress and a pair of court shoes, Marian looked at me expectantly.

'Lovely!' I replied, feeling very unsure.

'You're like a punk kid Lu,' Marian would tell me. 'But we need to smarten you up a bit.'

But while part of me resisted my new style, I also welcomed it because I wanted to fit into this world of people with cut-glass accents and English childhoods. I didn't want to be the scrappy kid anymore. Marian looked expensive and I wanted to look expensive too. Bit by bit, Marian polished my rough edges.

And as sophisticated as she was, Marian also wasn't cold and unattainable in the way I found some English people to be. She was warm, supportive and as inclusive to the Luvvers boys as she was to me. Plus, she had a great sense of humour. When we upgraded our old touring van to a Commer with precious heating as well as our own driver – a wonderful guy called Chris Cooke – she'd looked at him and smiled.

'I'm so pleased I've finally got someone to speak English with,' Marian had deadpanned.

But also, crucially for me, she had her head screwed on about money and got me one of the most respected accountants in London. Most importantly, she also realised how homesick and unhappy I was, however much I tried to hide it. And so, a few months after 'Shout' was released, with a busy performance and travelling schedule, she suggested I make a more permanent move to London. Her parents, a wonderful couple called Janey and Alf Gordon, had a spare room in their two-bedroom flat in St John's Wood and Marian knew they'd look after me well. Janey and Alf were empty nesters. I was missing home. It was the perfect match. The Luvvers meanwhile could move into a flat in nearby Queensway.

My parents agreed – Betty admittedly through gritted teeth – and I was soon installed in Janey and Alf's second bedroom. I loved both of them immediately. Janey was tiny, blonde and as glamorous as her daughter, while Alf wore a trilby, starched shirt and suit. Even at home. They were both so warm and kind. Plus, they had a bathroom, with hot water, and a cleaning lady called Bridie who I adored and would go on to work for me for twenty years.

For the first time in my life, I wasn't the one constantly running around after everybody. (Although I did still go to the Luvvers' flat every so often to do their washing because I was like Pavlov's dog when it came to housework.) My laundry was done, my clothes ironed and I soon learned about everything from gefilte fish and chopped liver, to the schmutter business. I knew nothing about Jewish culture before I moved in with Janey and Alf, but soon fell in love with it – I was drawn to the food, the sense of family and the desire to be the best version of yourself.

I was lucky to have Marian in so many ways. She protected me, guided me and created a safety net around me that wasn't just practical, it was emotional too. And I desperately needed that because while my family was filled with a lot of love, there were secrets too that had left me desperate for guidance and direction.

II

# 9

# Ur Eddie Likes a
# Good Drink . . . Wink, Wink

When I was a child, the only time I saw my grandfather, Eddie Lawrie Senior, he was sitting on the pavement, bottle clutched in his shaking hand. Or he'd wait on a street corner wearing an old overcoat my father had bought him until we passed and Dad dropped money into his pocket. Staring down at the pavement, I'd pray that no one we knew saw me.

Eddie Snr and my dad had long been estranged and both my parents refused to have anything to do with him beyond paying for his Salvation Army bed each week. Apparently, Betty had once tried to help, taking Eddie Snr in and drying him out. But his alcoholism was so severe, my grandfather had stolen from my parents, drunk it all away and, when my mother found him lying in urine-soaked sheets, she knew she couldn't cram all that under our tiny roof. Eddie Snr left and was never invited back.

Having grown up with alcoholism, it was all but inevitable that my father would also turn to alcohol because that was how it was for many families around us, generation after generation. And Eddie's black-market offal business also gave him the perfect excuse to visit the pub because that's where he conveniently did all his business. Surely, he needed to keep track as the butchers came in to order a pint that cost a couple of shillings, hand over a £10 note and leave without change? Once the landlord had taken his cut, the rest of the money went to Dad and he drank quite a lot of it.

But it meant that just as music and laughter were part of our family life, so was my father's constant drinking, which caused terrible conflict in our home. Not that we thought of it as an addiction, of course. I'd heard the word 'alcoholic', but we were too ashamed to use it. It was far easier to say that Eddie 'likes a good drink'. It was never openly talked about. I just knew that, most days, we'd get home from school to find Eddie back from the pub and sleeping it off. One of my pet hates, though, were the days when he hadn't got back and my mother would send me to the pub to find him.

'Can you ask my daddy to come home please?' I'd say at the pub door before running back home to find Mum waiting for me, alert, anxious and angry.

'Were his eyes small?' she'd ask.

'I don't know. I didn't see him Mammy. They said they'd send him home.'

Waiting for Eddie to get back, I'd feel Betty's nervous rage pouring out of her wordlessly and, while my dad had somehow taught himself not to lurch when he walked in our front door, his eyes would always betray him and my mother would follow, spitting with resentment.

'What is wrong with you?' she'd hiss. 'You cannot go a day without booze?'

'For Christ's sake, shut up,' Eddie would bark back. 'Can you not stop nagging me?'

But my mother could never not have the last word.

'You're useless Eddie Lawrie,' she'd screech. 'Why do you do it?'

On other days, my dad would fall asleep by the fire with a cigarette in his hand and Betty would berate him for nearly setting the place alight. Or he'd wake up hungover, irritable and ready for a fight. Lurching over to the fridge, Dad would pull open the door to see it packed with meat as my mother heated up some baked beans on the stove.

'Can you not cook a proper fuckin' meal woman?' he'd snap.

And that would be it. The tinderbox was lit, the insults would start, the screaming, the blame. And me in the middle of them, an eldest child desperate to keep the peace. I was convinced my family was different. Worse than everyone else's. I was ashamed of both the fights and my father's drinking. So, as a young girl, I decided that if I was good enough, and helpful enough, I could make things right. Everyone always told me how capable I was and I wanted to use the wiles I had developed to calm down the tension.

And the way to do that was by looking after our home. It wasn't that Betty was lazy. She was always knitting and busy with her hands. But, just as she wasn't that interested in cooking, she didn't seem to see the need for much tidying either. Every cupboard or drawer overflowed, which drove me wild. I'd see what my friends' homes looked like when I went to visit them – clean, tidy, ironing neatly stacked – and didn't dare invite anyone back to mine.

By the age of about seven or eight, I had taught myself how to scrub the floors, clean the kitchen, keep the staircase clean, iron shirts and make sure Billy washed behind his ears. Later on, I'd get up with Edwina and Gordon too, and feed and change them. In fact, I was so good at it all that Eddie gave me a nickname: Mrs Maclean. I'd go to the pawn shop too when money was tight because Betty couldn't face the neighbours' looks. Or to the Steamy, a vast public laundry filled with giant tubs.

'Oh, is your mother not coming today Marie?' the local women would say when they saw me turn up with a huge pram full of washing.

'Edwina's got a cold,' I would reply, defending Betty at all costs.

Cigarettes hanging out of often toothless mouths, the women would give me a knowing nod. After Edwina was born, Betty found it hard to get out of bed in the mornings, which meant I was on the go even more. Today, we know it as postnatal depression, but it was undiagnosed back then, so I learned to always smile and do whatever it took. A perfectionist streak was created inside me as I tried to create control in place of chaos.

Emotionally too, I was more parent than child because I was my mother's confidante, there to reassure Betty as she leaned on me. There was a lot of love, of course. Betty was my mother and she taught us that family was everything. But I was also the one who took the brunt of her insecurities, and they weren't just down to my father's drinking.

When Betty was a teenager, a stranger had turned up in the school playground and told her she was her 'real' sister. My mother had no idea what the girl was talking about. But, soon, dribs and drabs of a story started to be told. My grandparents, Nellie and Wullie McDonald, were in fact Betty's adoptive parents and had taken her in as a baby in return for an annual retainer. She'd been handed over to them by her biological grandmother, a staunch Protestant who was incensed by her daughter's marriage to a Catholic boy. My mother's biological parents had had five children together, but Betty was born while her father was in prison and her mother unwell. Seeing a chance, Betty's grandmother had taken her and given her to Nellie and Wullie, a good Protestant family, and no one had ever told Betty.

She was very loved, but the knowledge that she was the only one 'chosen' to be given up created a void of shame and sadness inside my mother that didn't completely heal until she was in her sixties. She lived for many years with a deep sense of not being good enough and, when she found out after their wedding that my father had had an earlier, very brief, first marriage, it further wounded her. Nothing was truly hers. So when I was born following a couple of miscarriages, Betty clung on to me like a life raft, never letting me out of her sight and leaning on me for everything.

The neediness inside my mother made me feel so claustrophobic that, at times, I'd push her away with one hand, while stepping in to fill the gap she left behind the other. Crucially, I also learned to be malleable and perform as much in my own home as I did on stage. On the outside, bright and confident; on the inside, compliant, anxious and trying to keep the peace, but hidden even to myself as I tried to juggle my parents' moods and emotions.

That's why I adapted so quickly after 'Shout'. I did what I'd always done for Marian, the music execs and journalists: threw myself in, refused to be intimidated, became what I thought people wanted me to be. I'd been handed an opportunity to leave the pain and shame of my past behind, so I happily stepped into the character created for me. And I loved my family too, so I wanted to make the most of an opportunity for us all when the money started to roll in soon after 'Shout' became a hit. My family had never been as poor as some, but life still felt unsafe and unpredictable. To teenage me, suddenly earning more money than I'd ever seen before, it seemed that I'd found a new way to fix what I'd spent so long trying to make right.

# 10

# People Are Watching You Now

The Luvvers and I had just done a gig, walked off stage and I was livid. I can't remember where we were or what exactly had happened. All I know is that I felt the boys had been lazy as we performed and I wasn't happy.

'It's not good enough,' I shouted as we stood in the wings of the venue. 'You're all staring at your feet and I'm up at the front giving it everything I've got while you're standing at the back.

'Give me a break, help me out here. Don't just leave it all to me.'

I might have been younger than the Luvvers, but they knew I wanted us to do our best every time we performed and, as biddable as I was with the record execs, the band was a different story. They were like brothers to me. I felt safe with them.

Walking up to our lead guitarist Ross, I started shoving him to get his attention.

'You're up there looking like you'd rather be in the pub,' I yelled. 'It's not just me performing. It's all of us. You wouldn't catch Keith Richards ignoring Mick Jagger would you?'

Ross scowled. And then he tutted.

That was it.

I shoved him, frustrated that he wasn't taking me seriously. But then I glanced at Marian and saw that her eyes were out on stalks. What was she looking so surprised at? Stopped in my tracks, I looked around at the boys and they stared back. Then we all started laughing. Didn't Marian know that's how we did things back in Glasgow? When we ran out of words, we got physical.

The boys wandered off to start packing up as Marian stood looking seriously at me.

'We need to talk Lu,' she said. 'People want to know everything about you now. They're watching you like a hawk. You can say what you want in a dressing room or the van, but not in front of strangers.'

'What do you mean?' I asked.

'You're in the newspapers Lu, on television,' Marian replied. 'You're on a pedestal now. People are fascinated. They want to know everything about you. So if you come across as angry or a spoiled brat, that's all they'll talk about. You have to protect yourself. Imagine if someone saw you yelling at Ross like that.'

'The boys don't care,' I said through gritted teeth.

'You're going to be judged for how you behave. And the last thing we want is you getting known as a bossy female.'

Embarrassment filled me as Marian spoke. I didn't want people thinking badly of me. I was just worried about the music. The people who'd paid to see us. That's what I cared about.

'I know the band understands you,' said Marian, more gently. 'But trust me, you've got to be careful how you behave now. They're grown men. You're just a girl. What will people think?'

I looked at my feet, trying to push down the feeling of shame that was making my skin feel hot and my ears buzz. In moments like this, I felt so far from home. Where I grew up, you had to stand your ground and fight your corner to protect what and who you loved. We'd grown up in an area where knives – and worse – were carried, and I'd learned to defend Billy so well that even the biggest kids in his school didn't dare touch him.

'Marie Lawrie's his sister,' they'd say if anyone went near him. 'She'll batter you.'

I never actually hit anyone. But I had convinced them I would with a tough attitude and a look that warned anyone off.

'See that face?' Betty would cry if she saw me scowl. 'If that face freezes, you'll go to hell Marie.'

The only person I ever actually laid a finger on was a boy called Whitey who was a member of the Tongs, one of the two main gangs in our area. Even though he was just a kid, Whitey could usually be found with a knife, iron bar or axe.

Weapons aside, I liked him.

I'd known Whitey – and boys like him – all my life. But, one day, Billy had come home with blood on his face after going out for ice cream and my blood was up for Whitey, who I was sure had hit him. After searching the local area, I found Whitey and grabbed him by the collar, roaring as I pushed him against a wall.

'Try it again,' I shouted. 'And you'll see what you'll get.'

Whitey had just smiled at me – and then taken Billy to find the boys who'd actually hit him and made my brother fight back.

But now I listened quietly as Marian spoke to me about dirty laundry and airing it in public, keeping my anger private, being in the spotlight and having to behave accordingly. Feeling chastened, I got into the van for the drive back to London and thought about what she had said. Marian was right. I was lucky I had her to teach me how to do things right because I was in a different world now. And it was time to learn its rules.

# 11

# Back Home, They Think We're Rich

Sitting in Janey and Alf's flat, I twirled the phone cable around my finger as my mother talked.

'I needed to get to the shops today but I couldn't get out,' she said. 'My hair wasn't done and I can't leave the house like that now that you're a pop star Marie.'

'Don't worry about all that,' I replied as I tried to calm Betty down. 'It doesn't matter. Nothing's really changed.'

'Nothing's changed?' she exclaimed. 'You're in the newspapers Marie. On the television. Sheila Campbell asked me last week why we're still living here when you're in the charts and living in London? I didn't know where to put myself. They think we're rich now.'

The first thing I'd done after getting an accountant was to make sure money was sent back to Glasgow to cover all the bills, but it wasn't growing on trees quite yet.

'I'm sorry Mammy,' I said gently. 'I know it's hard for you.'

'Do you?' Betty replied. 'We hardly ever see you these days.'

Silence.

'How are the weans?' I asked tentatively and listened as my mother started reeling off the ins and outs of the day.

Gordon had skinned his knees at school, Edwina was doing well at her dance classes and Billy had had an awful fight with Dad. My brother was almost a teenager now and I worried constantly that Eddie would bully him. I also knew Betty was struggling. I could hear it in her voice and the way Billy spoke on the phone.

'She's okay,' he'd say whenever I asked how Mum was.

'Are you sure?'

'Stop worrying. We're alright.'

'And Dad?'

'Same.'

I understand now, of course, how my mother felt. I know the wrench of your child growing up and away from you. And at a time when most kids we knew stayed in Glasgow, rooted to their parents' orbit and close to family forever, it hurt her when I left. But Betty's unhappiness made her whine and needle constantly, and I felt torn, missing home, wanting to phone to hear their voices, but also somehow relieved that I was not there because every call left me feeling guilty.

The trouble with being mentored by Marian – and lapping up every lesson – was that my mother resented it. She made no bones about her hurt, upset and anger that Marian had become so important to me. Not that she said it out loud, of course. It was just there hanging between us when I phoned home every night to tell her every detail of what we'd done, what I'd worn and what Marian had said.

'So she's letting you go out at night now is she?' my mother would snap. 'To nightclubs? At your age?'

'I'm always with the band Mammy. I just have a Coke, and Janey and Alf stay up to see me home.'

But nothing could soothe the Betty's resentment that she'd been replaced. No matter that I was a teenager plunged into a new world who needed guidance, Betty felt abandoned and wasn't going to forgive me easily.

# 12

# Under Pressure

Having a big hit single creates expectation. And pressure. 'Shout' could only take us so far and the Luvvers and I needed to follow it up to avoid being dismissed as a one-hit wonder. I was also aware of the whispers around me in the industry and music press that I only had one song, and style, in me. I even heard one person say that if I kept singing as I did, I wouldn't have a voice for much longer. So three months after 'Shout' entered the charts, we released our second single, once again produced by Peter Sullivan. The song was called 'Can't Hear You No More' and co-written by Carole King. But when it failed to chart, I was even more determined to prove the doubters wrong.

Decca decided to try a new approach and assigned Bert Berns, a legendary American writer and producer who'd produced hits for artists including the Drifters and Ben E. King at Atlantic and also co-written 'Twist and Shout'. I felt ecstatic to be working with him as we recorded his song 'Here Comes the Night' which was released in late 1964.

'I think I'm just a very lucky girl,' I told a reporter from the *Record Mirror*. 'Here I am, only just sixteen, and look at all the wonderful things that are happening.

'People say I should go back to the "Shout" sort of stuff, but finding another "Shout" isn't so easy. I really want to be thought of as a versatile singer and I do love singing soulful ballads.'

All I wanted was to prove that I was a 'real' singer. Show the industry I had so much more in me. But the track didn't land with the record-buying public and 'Here Comes the Night' crawled into the charts at number fifty. When Bert soon rerecorded it with a young singer called Van Morrison and his band Them, their version of the song – far better than mine – reached number two four months later. And I felt completely crushed.

# 13

# Play It Again

I knew what music I wanted to sing because it spoke to the deepest part of me and all the emotions buried there. My dad was the one who always brought new seventy-eights home, and I was serenaded in the crib by Perry Como, Matt Monro, Ella Fitzgerald and Frank Sinatra. But the first voice I can vividly remember shaking me to my core was Big Mama Thornton's as she sang 'Hound Dog'. I had no idea what a hound dog was. All I knew was that the sound coming out of the record player felt like it was reaching inside me, churning me up and spitting me out.

Mama Thornton's voice was powerful, urgent. I'd never heard a woman attack music like she did. Mama Thornton was different and played a mean guitar. I just didn't understand what all the fuss was about when Elvis released his version a few years later.

Day after day, I'd sit with my ear pressed to the speaker, listening to her again and again, picking up the needle and dropping it back to hear this phrase or that, wedging myself tight against the sound to hear every inflection. It felt like I was listening to someone digging into their soul and pulling what they found out into the open for everyone to experience. This was what I loved about American music.

Everything changed again when I heard Ray Charles. The emotion he expressed, the way he told the story. I felt his pain and it was as if he was communicating directly to my soul. This is why some artists rise above all others to become great. Within just a few notes, they can create an emotional connection with each one of us that feels unique. For me, it was Big Mama Thornton first. Then Ray. Later Otis Redding. And B.B. King as well, to mention just a few. Their phrasing, their intonation, the raw interpretation was so different from the clinical British way of singing. We copied the Americans, but their authenticity and originality tapped into something deep inside.

Like many Glaswegians at the time, I looked west to America for music and films, not south to England. The clipped voices of English singers like Petula Clark or Helen Shapiro didn't resonate with me. But the ones from America – particularly those of black singers – did. And something inside me connected to the raw feeling they communicated because my childhood had created so many emotions I did not know what to do with. This music allowed those feelings to flow outwards just a little at a time when no one ever spoke about feelings.

My mother also inspired my passion for America because Betty wasn't interested in the English cut-glass accent of films like *The Bridge on the River Kwai* or *The Ladykillers* on our regular cinema trips. But give her anything that Rock Hudson was in and she was happy as a clam. After going to the green grocer to pick up half a dozen oranges, she'd sit popping slices into her mouth as she devoured *Some Like It Hot* and *Sunset Boulevard* with us beside her. My dad, meanwhile, was all about the music and I grew up at a time when rhythm and blues, soul and gospel were beginning to move from the fringes into mainstream music where they influenced so many Sixties artists.

Everyone in Glasgow was the same. The record shops were full of imports. And by the time I was a young teen, the Luvvers had introduced me to artists like John Lee Hooker and Muddy Waters, the Drifters, Sam Cooke, Solomon Burke and the Isley Brothers, who wrote 'Shout'. I was hooked and felt the same when I saw *West Side Story* complete with working-class kids in rival gangs, just like the ones I'd grown up with – raw and powerful singing and dancing.

All of this, the music and film, soaked into me – even if my dad wasn't so keen on some of the new voices I brought into our home.

'Just sounds like he's moanin',' he said every time I put on Ray Charles.

Hearing 'Shout' for the first time gave me the same kind of feeling. The Luvvers and I had gone to see Alex Harvey at a club in town and knew he'd just been to Hamburg like the Beatles. Thin as a rake and dressed in black leather, Alex had walked onto the stage and done an amazing rendition of 'Shout' and I was enthralled. The rock influences, the notes that I could open up my voice around, the raw emotion I could channel into it – everything I couldn't articulate in conversation expressed in the music.

Because, even as a child, there was just one thing I was sure of: I had to sing. And the music that moved me when I was young was also the music I aspired to make as I grew up.

Powerful, emotional, meaningful.

# 14

# A Beatle at the Window

Watching in horror as Dog, my tiny Yorkshire terrier, tried to mount Paul McCartney's huge old English sheepdog Martha as we stood chatting on Janey and Alf's doorstep was the moment I knew I'd crossed from Kansas into Oz.

I'd first met Paul and the rest of the band after being invited to the Beatles' Christmas Show at the Hammersmith Odeon at the end of 1964. Standing in the wings, I'd watched the boys run off – and back on – the stage as the sound of screaming almost took off the roof.

'Oh it's Lulu,' Paul and John exclaimed in their thick Liverpool accent when they rushed past me.

I'd just turned sixteen and hearing the Beatles use my name out loud made me want to faint. When a few of us were invited back to the boys' dressing room, I watched breathlessly as Paul stuck his head under a tap to wet *that* hair. The sink was cracked and stained, the dressing room tiny and cramped. I thought the Beatles would get better treatment than that. All thoughts of time forgotten, I didn't get back to Janey and Alf's until almost dawn.

'I thought you'd been kidnapped,' Janey exclaimed as I walked into the flat. 'I've been up all night worried sick.'

'You won't believe it!' I yelped. 'The Beatles invited me back to their party!'

Janey, who usually loved hearing all about the people I was meeting, was too preoccupied by how late I was to be impressed. But even she had to give a second glance when the world's biggest pop star started stopping for a chat occasionally. Paul didn't live far from Janey and Alf's flat, and walked Martha in a nearby park. I'd also got to know him a bit out and about after that first meeting at the Odeon, or doing different shows together. Then, one day, I heard a knock on the window and looked up to see him standing outside. I nearly jumped out of my skin. A Beatle? Wanting to talk to me?

From then on, Paul would stop and chat sometimes when he was on a walk and it was during one of those visits that my Yorkie ended up getting overcome with passion. As Paul roared with laughter, I died ever so slowly of embarrassment.

What I quickly realised, though, is that people are just people – however stratospheric their fame. Back in Glasgow, I had assumed 'fame' was like another, very special, planet and somehow everyone on it was different. But even geniuses are human, I was beginning to realise. And by the time Paul and I had got to know each other, my crush was also a distant memory because the night I'd first met the Beatles, I'd also seen Eric Clapton play for the first time with the Yardbirds.

I'd bumped into Eric early on at the Marquee Club in Soho and hadn't taken much notice of him. But seeing him perform changed everything. He was like a god on stage – his musicality, his physicality. Being hair-obsessed, I'd decided that his was even better than Paul's. It took years to shake off the rolling waves of nervy sickness that filled me every time Eric was around, but I was so awkward, I had to stand at the other end of the room pretending that he didn't matter.

'How's Eric?' Paul would ask with a grin whenever we were all in a club or at a gig together, and my face would go beetroot.

'No one else got a look in,' Jack Bruce, Cream's singer and bass guitarist, told me later. 'We didn't even try because you were so into Eric.'

Not that I thought I stood a chance with him or any of them. I was a kid. They were in their twenties. Just a few years at that age feels like a chasm. They were all so out of reach. And most of them treated me like a little sister. All I cared about was that they seemed to like my voice. I wanted to be respected. Not seduced.

And, Beatles aside, most of the people I was getting to know didn't have a clue where their music was headed. The names might mean something today, but, back then, we were all work-ing it out as we went along. Yusuf Islam, or Cat Stevens as he was then, would appear at Janey and Alf's often to play me his new stuff. He'd soon have his first hit with 'I Love My Dog'. Others were already established, and Mick Jagger had sauntered up after we'd appeared on the same bill at the Queen's Hall in Leeds.

'Allo Lulu,' he'd drawled, looking me up and down.

I wasn't quite sure if he was nice or not. Mick felt a bit too dangerous for me. And my childhood had taught me that if you sensed danger then it was best to stay far away. . . Not engage.

# 15

# Rollercoaster

My music career felt like a roller coaster; I never liked them.

Decca were chasing another hit, but we were led down many paths and most of them were wrong. I recorded a song written by Mick Jagger and Keith Richards, given to me by their manager Andrew Loog Oldham, that failed to chart. Next came 'Leave a Little Love' which got to number eight and stayed in the Top Forty for the next couple of months, so it felt like we were on the up again. Three months later, 'Try to Understand' got to number twenty-five, which was okay, but felt like a flop to me. Up. Down. Up. Down. Professionally. And emotionally too.

Chart hits were enough to keep my profile high, but I'd never aspired to be 'famous'. All I wanted was to sing, make music and develop as an artist. But being a very small, very white Glaswegian meant I'd also quickly been cast by music execs and the media as a young girl-next-door type. I didn't have the edgy look, or middle-class rebellious streak, that propelled others, and the record men seemed unsure about what to do with me after 'Shout'. The sound I was drawn to – rock infused with soul, R&B, gospel and blues – didn't fit my physical appearance, which straitjacketed women then even more than it does today.

Also, I was young. So young. And in an industry dominated by men – not just the ones out front performing, but those running the labels and studios too – I felt too intimidated by many of them and their achievements to insist on being the artist I wanted to be in the way others did. My gender, my background and my childhood had all left me feeling 'less than' deep down inside. I felt like there was a learner plate stuck on my back and the fact that I could sing pretty much anything thrown at me was also a problem – as was the fact that I agreed to do it all, never dreaming I could say no. Still being the good girl. Still keeping quiet. Doing as I was told, just as I'd learned through all the years of my father's drinking and my mother's unhappiness; never daring to stand up and insist on what I felt was right for me to studio execs who were so much older. And so, as dominant as I was when I performed, I was a small young woman who couldn't get my opinions heard. At the same time, desperately anxious to please and blessed with a voice that I could morph to most kinds of sound.

If only I'd had a bit more of Dusty's experience and determination to have her opinions taken seriously.

I hero-worshipped her as her star rose and rose. Dusty was focused and knew what she wanted. But she was also almost a decade older than me and had had time to hone her sound to understand what worked for her. I'd never got that chance doing covers as a kid. Who knows what might have been if I'd had my first hit just a few years later with a bit more time to really explore my music?

Marian did her best to build my career. And she served me so well in many ways. She kept me safe and financially stable, but she was also one of very few women in the industry and didn't have a background in the recording industry. The Beatles were the Beatles, plus they had Brian Epstein and, because of their worldwide success, he had respect from the men in suits. The Stones had Andrew Loog Oldham who was a master at strategy. People might think solo artists rise out of the fire of their own talent, and some do of course. But many are propelled by either a key creative partnership or a team around them – Artists & Repertoire (A&R) men and producers finding the right tracks, plus managers with a vision. Marian was driven and fierce. But she, too, was a woman in a man's world learning in real time, just like me, and there was no plan. We didn't know if any of it was going to last past the next single. And so, we ran with opportunities when they came.

From the start, Marian saw how the public had responded to me. I didn't shuffle on stage and 'just' sing. I performed, connected to a crowd, and Marian believed I could create a career as an all-round entertainer, which is why TV felt like a natural next step. After appearing on a primetime BBC pop show called *Gadzooks! It's the In Crowd* with the Luvvers, I'd been asked back to present it. Cathy McGowan had held her own on *Ready Steady Go!* with no experience, Marian reasoned. She was sure I could do the same.

Like I said, Marian had blind faith.

For me, it was all such a whirl that I never stepped back to look clearly at the horizon and was always prepared to try new things, however terrified I felt. I'd learned to fake a brazen attitude from the cradle after all. And I desperately wanted to be the person Marian believed I was – I would do anything to make her happy and proud. So I swallowed my nerves and got in front of a TV camera aged sixteen to co-host *Gadzooks!* for a few episodes, introducing everyone from the Animals and the Who, to Roger Whittaker and Peter and Gordon.

Quite the mix.

# 16

# Behind the Iron Curtain

Two years on from 'Shout', the gigs had got bigger and bigger, I was constantly performing, on TV and, between us, the Luvvers and I were earning good money. Because while my chart performance was up and down, 'Shout' had been a huge hit, I'd had other records in the charts and was still in the media so much that appetite was high for my performances. I was also regularly winning awards from the music press.

In March 1966, I hit the headlines again when the Luvvers and I toured Poland with the Hollies because I was one of the first female artists to go behind the Iron Curtain. Skipping off a plane onto the tarmac in Communist Poland wearing a pink fur coat with matching pale pink patent boots and hair bow did not seem remotely incongruous to me at the time. But wearing this outfit as I stepped onto the tarmac in grey, war-scarred, economically deprived Sixties Warsaw was a little tone deaf I realise now. And while I'd been expecting plush hotels and room service, I soon realised not in Poland. There were bullet holes in walls, damaged buildings and debris. The hotels were grey and dour, and the food matched the décor.

The strangest thing, though, was performing to a crowd of

teenagers surrounded by stony-faced guards who stepped forwards menacingly if anyone looked as if they might be about to enjoy themselves. In fact, when a young boy approached the stage and offered me a small bouquet of flowers, a guard hit his hands with a truncheon and broke his fingers, I found out later. We tried to get spirits high. But it's hard when your audience isn't allowed to stand up or applaud. Compared to the screaming and mayhem we'd had in Britain, it felt like we were at a wake.

Graham Nash, who was then with the Hollies, was incensed by the whole thing. I, meanwhile, spent all the złotys we were given for our per diem – the first time we'd ever got one – calling home because I still felt so lonely.

There was sadness too when we got back to the UK because the Luvvers and I split. It had been a while coming. Everyone – from Decca to the press – had focused on me, and a lot of the music had been released under my name alone. The band had continued to tour and perform with me, but session musicians had been used more and more in the studio. Understandably, it had frustrated the boys and we'd started to grow apart. I wanted to hold us together, I really did, and I tried hard to, but I couldn't. I felt sad about the end of the band, and really torn. I knew I owed the Luvvers a huge debt. I would never have dared to do all I'd done without them. But, deep down, I also knew I could not hold us together.

I was now a solo artist.

III

# 17

# The One About My Hair Colour

The moments which change things profoundly are often the ones you hardly notice. In my case, it was a disagreement about my hair which veered my life onto a different course.

Marian's sister Felice worked for the famous acting agent John Heyman, who looked after people like Richard Burton and Liz Taylor, and had heard a director was looking for a mix of young actors for a film he was casting. I could sing and present – why not try acting?

'Are you jokin'?' I said to Marian when she suggested I audition. 'I haven't got a clue.'

Marian, as ever, wouldn't hear a word of it. The director was called James Clavell – he'd written films including *The Great Escape* and would go on to write bestsellers including *Noble House* and *Shōgun*, and he was now going to produce and direct his new script with a big Hollywood star.

'Perfect, it's a great opportunity,' Marian told me. 'You will be a great actress. Plus, any director will know that having you in their film will be an asset.'

Marian was right. My profile was still riding high thanks to touring, press interviews and appearances on shows like

*Morecambe and Wise* and *Juke Box Jury*. And so, soon after Marian and I had talked, James Clavell came to see me backstage after a show.

'We'll need to change the colour of your hair,' he declared, towering over me.

Who did he think he was? I loved my red hair. And if Betty had taught me one thing, it was never to mess with good hair when you finally had it.

The hair colour I became so known for had happened by accident when I was about fourteen. My mother's biological sister, Margaret, who was quite a character and extremely attractive, had visited us from Canada. With red hair and a swan-like neck, Aunt Margaret kept telling me that I looked just like her and, while I was doubtful that I was pretty like her, it gave me the idea to go to the hairdresser for a subtle rinse to brighten up my mousy locks. Somehow, my hair had turned the colour of autumn leaves by the time the towel came off.

The hairdresser was almost as shocked as I was. I loved it.

'For gawd's sake,' Betty had screamed when I got home. 'Wait until your daddy sees you.'

Eddie had indeed hit the roof. But he wasn't the only one who was incensed. When I got into school on Monday, my headmistress – who, in my memory at least, was a horrifying cross between Miss Hannigan and Miss Trunchbull – had thundered towards me at the end of assembly.

'I suppose you think this is going to make the boys like you with that hair?' she hissed.

'No, Miss,' I replied.

She bent down closer to me.

'You think this makes you look attractive?'

'No, Miss.'

Turning on her heel, she'd fetched a jar of disinfectant, which permanently housed a nit comb, and made me drag it through my hair, leaving me dripping, mortified and humiliated. Her school was considered the best in the area and I presume she wanted to take an upstart local teen singer down a peg or two. Apparently, some of my classmates felt the same way because one had beaten me up in an alleyway soon after I'd started at the school. I always felt like the odd one out, especially as I would burst into song at every opportunity. Some liked it, some didn't. But all this, plus the constant demands of home, meant getting disinfected was the last straw for me and I cut class more and more after that. Eventually, I was transferred to a less prestigious school because I wasn't keeping up, but, in truth, I gave up on education long before I left it – losing my nerve when I left in the mornings and looking up to Betty at the flat window. Face contorting, I'd silently plead with her as she stared down at me.

'Please Mammy,' I'd whisper. 'Please, please let me stay off.'

It never took long. Betty would usually relent in under a minute if it meant having company, and she'd summon me back upstairs with a jerk of her head and finger pressed to her lips to instruct me to be quiet so the neighbours wouldn't know what was going on.

'You're gonna get me killed one day Marie Lawrie,' she'd say as I walked back in.

Within minutes, I'd either have a baby on my hip or a brush in my hand as Betty settled down beside the fire to knit. I came to realise that knitting was my mother's meditation.

Neither my headmistress nor my classmates needed to have gone to all that trouble to cut me down. Pretty was not a word I'd have used about myself. And I never, ever, thought I was any better than the rest. But I did like my hair. And I was not going to change it. Film or no film. I didn't care who this director was.

The fierce look I gave James Clavell that day, however, must have convinced him he could do something with me in the film because soon Marian called in excitement.

'He's written you into the film and I've done a deal where you also sing the title song.'

I was amazed and anxious in equal measure.

'You'll only be on £100 a week but we know why you're doing this. It's not for the money.'

And the film?

It was called *To Sir, With Love.*

# 18

# I Am a Lady, I Am

'We want Lulu!' a crowd of kids chanted when I arrived on location in East London in the spring of 1966.

But however excited they were to see me, I felt like a total imposter in my new world. Again.

James Clavell had gathered the cast together a week before filming started to help us get to know each other and form real relationships which would transfer onto screen. It had worked because all of us were young and dizzy with anticipation, and quickly created a rapport.

But the trouble for me was that everyone seemed to have gone to stage school and I didn't have a clue. Worse, they were all English and could easily flip into a Cockney accent. I knew I'd stick out like a sore thumb if I sounded Scottish. I spent the entire week listening like a hawk and going home to practise my London accent until it became believable.

I was playing Barbara Pegg. Mouthy. Cheeky. So far, so familiar. But I still felt completely out of my depth and the arrival of a huge movie star on set didn't help either. Sidney Poitier came to London on the back of winning a best actor Academy Award for *Lilies of the Field*. The first African American man to win one. He'd made history and I was fascinated by him. Sidney was so exact, contained and sophisticated. While the rest of us milled around between takes, Sidney would either work with his acting coach or sit reading the six newspapers he got every day. I didn't even read one.

I was intrigued by how similar he was to his on-screen character too. Sidney had that same quiet but authoritative air that demanded respect. Plus, I was in awe of him and slightly terrified. So, on a rare afternoon when he stayed on set in between takes, he opened up for the first time and I felt the need to try to charm him.

'I love your wife Diahann Carroll,' I said in a rush.

Sidney looked as me so coolly, I almost felt the Arctic blast.

'She isn't my wife,' he said as his gaze shifted from shocked to bemused.

I'd been quietly – but firmly – put back in my box and later realised why. Diahann Carroll was Sidney's lover and he'd just divorced his actual wife Juanita Hardy.

If I'd thought for longer than ten seconds, I wouldn't have been surprised he kept to himself. We were a bunch of teenagers. Sidney was thirty-nine. A huge star. He was in a different league. This was an important project for him and he was all business.

A combination of managing to mimic the accent and forcing myself to ad lib my way through my nervousness meant my small role grew a little larger after filming started as James encouraged me to improvise.

'Who's she bleedin' think she is?' I chirped in one scene as Sidney's character Mark Thackeray chatted to a female teacher.

James leapt on the idea that Barbara, and all the other girls, had a crush on him – a potentially incendiary idea back then. Not long after *To Sir* came out, Petula Clark touched Harry Belafonte's hand on a TV show and it caused a scandal in America. The very idea that a white girl or woman could be romantically interested in a black man was incredibly potent because, while the Sixties might have been known for breaking down boundaries, they were also still the Dark Ages in many ways.

The racial implications of the film, however, flew straight over my head. For me, *To Sir* was simply about a group of working-class kids gaining respect for a middle-class teacher who showed them something more. As my part grew, I was just relieved to be holding my own. And there was also something else on my mind that felt far more important: the title song.

I was going to have to sing it when we shot the end of the movie and, as the weeks slid by, I was getting more and more anxious about it. Marian and I had been expecting the studio – one of Hollywood's biggest – to come up with something great. They could surely get any songwriter they wanted. Sidney Poitier was starring. The movie needed a powerful song.

But we waited and waited, and nothing happened.

'What are they doing?' I kept asking Marian in nervous phone calls. 'The whole film closes with this song. Why aren't they doing anything?'

But no one apart from us seemed too bothered.

By now, Marian was also managing a Canadian comic called Mark London, who sang and wrote songs too. So, when I saw him at Marian's house one day, I had an idea.

'Why don't you have a go at writing the *To Sir* theme song?' I said.

Mark had looked at me in horror.

'They'll never go for it. They're not going to use a song by an unknown.'

'Well, they haven't got anything else,' I cried. 'Please Mark. Just try. You know what sounds right for me.'

He quickly came up with a melody, I tried it out and we polished it off together before we sent it to Don Black who we'd asked to write the lyrics. The whole thing only took a couple of days, so quite why the studio hadn't been able to do the same, I wasn't sure. But the producers agreed to use the song and, while *To Sir* wasn't my usual kind of sound, I loved it because the lyrics encapsulated the entire heart-wrenching message of the film.

Having gone solo, I'd also signed to a new label and was now at EMI where my new producer was a guy called Mickie Most who'd produced the Animals, as well as masterminded Herman's Hermits' success in the US. But when I went in to the studio with him to record *To Sir*, I could tell Mickie wasn't really into the whole thing and it frustrated me. I think he thought it was just a distraction from the 'real' music. Maybe he resented it. But while I had expected to have a thirty-piece orchestra playing the arrangement and making it soar, all we got was a rhythm section and a couple of strings.

'It's the climax to the whole film,' I said to Mickie. 'There's a really big scene at the end. We've all fallen in love with Sidney. He's turned us from snivelling kids to young adults.

'We need a big sound, like the title song from *Born Free*. Don Black wrote the lyrics for that too and it won an Academy Award for best original song.'

Mickie looked at me disinterestedly.

'Nah.'

We recorded the song and then all I could do was wait for the film to be released. But when I finally saw it at a pre-screening, I was horrified. I couldn't act. I looked ugly. My thoughts spiralled. What was Marian thinking when she agreed for me to do this? I looked like I was just making it up as I went along. When this film came out, I'd never live it down. The people making the movie had no idea what they were doing. It was going to be a disaster.

# 19

# But I've Got Spots

As I turned eighteen and 1966 segued into 1967, the Sixties were well and truly swinging and youth culture was building towards the Summer of Love. Drugs and sex pulsated around me in the music industry, but while the lid had been blown off any kind of reserve, I had no clue how to navigate it all. Anxious to fit in, make-up and clothes became ever more important to me, part of the character of 'Lulu' to hide behind.

While I'd been billed on posters as the 'wee belter' as a child, I'd become 'Little Miss Dynamite' by the time I was a teenager. Three small words that contained a world: young and innocent enough to be a 'miss', yet somehow also sexually available 'dynamite' because of my energy on stage and the way I moved. One record exec said I was 'no good' in long dresses.

'You need to see her hips moving nineteen to the dozen,' he added.

The press asked me endlessly about boyfriends, my love life was speculated on and I was described as a 'firecracker' and 'hot potato'. But, deep down, I was fiercely guarding a secret: it was all a mask.

I was still travelling constantly and had performed with Roy Orbison (captivated by a stage style so contained it was almost robotic until that voice came out) as well as the Walker Brothers (convinced I was in love with Scott by about day two as I stood by the side of the stage listening to him sing in that dark, rich tone). A few months later, I supported the Beach Boys, who were riding high on the success of their album *Pet Sounds* and their hit 'Good Vibrations', on their UK tour that saw fans go wild (entranced by their incredible harmonies night after night and mourning the fact that Brian Wilson wasn't with them because I'd dreamed that he might record me one day).

I also went back into the studio with Mickie to record new material, and our first track together, 'The Boat That I Row', was written by Neil Diamond. There are few better writers, and it got to number six. I was back up again. Mickie the hitmaker had worked his magic and soon Marian came to me with a proposal.

'They want you to be the new face of Lux soap,' she said.

'But Elizabeth Taylor has done it!' I replied.

'It'll be fine Lu!' Marian insisted.

'I'm not skinny enough. And I get spots.'

Marian smiled.

'Oh, darling. Good lighting and make-up will sort all that out. You think Hollywood stars wake up looking like that? There's so much they can do with film today. Trust me.'

Turning on her heel, Marian strode out of the room, no doubt to assure Lux I'd be delighted to star in their next campaign and get the contract signed by end of day. Whatever she said, though, I knew what beauty looked like – and it wasn't me. I was surrounded by women who unravelled endless legs out of cars before leaning forwards to light a cigarette with a swish of their mane; ethereal creatures beloved by most of the male musicians I knew. Tall, willowy models like Pattie Boyd and Jean Shrimpton or little Twiggy. Tiny, round-cheeked and very unwillowy me did not look like them in the slightest.

If one word summed me up aged eighteen, it was 'more': I wanted to be more tall, more thin, more beautiful. I'd tried a few diet pills to lose some weight, but ate even more than usual the moment they wore off. Being on the road so much didn't help either. It was chips, chips and more chips at most service stations. Or curries and chocolate. The battle with my teenage skin felt like a war of attrition as spots popped out, seemingly knowing when I was about to appear on TV or do a photo shoot.

Marian, however, knew why Lux wanted me: I was an every girl kind of girl, pretty but not too pretty, fashionable but not too out of reach. Soon the words 'Today's girl, today's look' were rolling across the screen for the Lux TV ad as I walked into shot wrapping a feather boa around my neck for some unfathomable reason. Looking into the camera, I spoke in my now perfectly English accent that sounded as if I'd grown up somewhere between Cheltenham and Chelsea. The erasure of Marie Lawrie, on the outside at least, was complete.

'Lux is so beautifully mild, I wouldn't trust my complexion to anything else,' I trilled as I looked into the lens.

The neighbours in Glasgow were horrified.

'Has she gone over to the other side with that accent of hers?' they'd say to Betty who'd report back to me down the phone, bristling with anger.

No one said anything when I went back home to visit, of course, but the people who just happened to 'drop in' when I was there – and there were a lot of them – must have seen how much I'd changed.

Being split between two different worlds certainly increased my anxiety, and self-doubt about how I looked wormed between the cracks of a life that was blessed in so many other ways. The loneliness of the early years, for instance, was far behind me and I now had a great group of girlfriends. Angela Cash was in the clothing business, Joanne Newfield was Brian Epstein's PA and I was also close to the Beatles' wives: Cynthia Lennon, Maureen Starkey and Pattie Boyd. Cyn was slightly older than me, an artist who'd become a reluctant celebrity and was shy and very kind. Maureen was a down-to-earth Liverpudlian hairdresser who dressed like a Goth, was fiercely independent and willing to speak her mind. Pattie was Pattie: beyond beautiful, soft, gentle and friendly. I loved them all.

Together, we existed in a whirl of money, fame and fans clamouring for autographs. On nights off, there were invites to parties and premieres, seats in roped-off VIP areas in nightclubs like The Scotch, Revolution and The Speakeasy, long dinners in restaurants such as Le Gavroche and clothes by designers like Mary Quant, Ossie Clark and Barbara Hulanicki. With an ever-increasing love of fashion plus money to spend, I shopped in London and Paris for a wardrobe that grew and grew. A teenager with more money than sense.

The problem, however, is that living in that kind of bubble doesn't wash away insecurities. In many ways, it only heightens them because you suddenly have something to lose. Marie hadn't imagined a future past a job as a hairdresser and kids by the age of eighteen. Lulu had the world at her feet. But tell-tale signs of my self-doubt slipped out of me like wisps of smoke trailing from embers – so delicate that even I didn't notice them.

I was now earning enough, for instance, to invest in property and had bought Betty and Eddie a two-bedroom flat in Dennistoun. My mother had chosen it and their new home had high ceilings, large windows and – of course – its own bathroom. I'd also bought myself a three-bedroom house in St John's Wood. With no less than three bathrooms. I couldn't get enough of them after all the washing in sinks as a kid.

But instead of asking someone my own age to live with me, a girlfriend to share clothes with, nights out and tales of the latest boyfriends, I invited Janey. That was partly because Alf had sadly died and I wanted to look after Janey because that's what I'd always done. But I think I wanted to be looked after too and Janey did that. Old beyond my years on one hand, stuck in childhood on the other.

I didn't stop to think about all that though. I just pushed on, busy, busy. But however many clothes I bought, make-up looks I tried or Lux contracts I got, my anxieties could not be completely contained. And there was one area in particular which made me feel very self-conscious: sex. It felt like a black hole pulling everyone around me in while I floated around in deep space watching them get swallowed up, which fed my feeling of being a step apart.

I had boyfriends of course. Alex Bell from the Luvvers was my first, and there was a brief romance with Peter Noone of

Herman's Hermits. But none of it went much further than a goodnight kiss because I'd skipped so much school that human biology had completely passed me by and, in those days, we didn't do the teenage conversations that you see in Hollywood films today which might have started to reveal its secrets. I didn't have a clue.

I was also no longer quite the little sister I had been when I started out, and some musicians certainly started to express interest in me. One even went so far as to trail me for hours in his expensive car as I shopped on Bond Street with my mum. Whenever we looked up, there he was, parked at the side of the road. Betty could tell that he was extremely enamoured of me, but I couldn't find the courage to say hello. Marian said that others were drawn to me because of my innocence, or had convinced themselves I was hiding a wild streak because of the way I moved on stage. After spending the evening necking with one musician, for instance, he'd looked at me in confusion after realising it wouldn't go any further.

'You're a virgin?' he'd said in a voice like a curious museum curator staring at a rare specimen.

I never had any bad experiences because I was protected by Marian and made sure to befriend musicians' wives and girl-friends as a way to both protect myself and show I wasn't interested. I was also always very clear that I didn't want to end up like one of the women who crowded around my male contemporaries like bees on honey. I wasn't a fan. I was a musician. But, the truth is, I was also afraid of sex. It had never been openly discussed in my home and Betty had made it seem almost shameful, one of the many threads that coursed through the black rage between my parents. I wanted love, I wanted romance. I was just scared of the reality, so I spent my time wrapped up in fantasy, in love with the idea of love.

My crush on Eric, however, still burned strong and I remained desperate to see him. So, one night, I threw a party and invited everyone – the Beatles, the Who, the Animals and Cat Stevens – hoping he'd come too. Nervously waiting for him to arrive, I kept an eye on the door until he finally walked in and then turned to chat animatedly to someone else in an effort to ignore him. But, late that night, we ended up outside smoking and, heart palpitating, I tried to act cool.

It obviously didn't work.

'So any boyfriends yet Lu?' Eric said. 'You need to get out there, find someone really nice.'

I felt my heart sink as he smiled at me with the kind of slightly embarrassed kindness that your older brother's best friend uses when they realise you idolise them. I'd never wished so hard for the ground to swallow me up. I thought I was playing my part so brilliantly: young, fun and certainly not inexperienced. But, apparently, Eric had seen through it. Or Paul bloody McCartney had said something to him.

But I just didn't realise how hopelessly naïve I was as everyone around me kicked against the rules while I was so crippled by modesty, I couldn't even go on stage wearing the wrong bra.

'Just go on without one,' Marian had said casually when I'd got to a gig and realised I'd brought black underwear and a white top.

She might as well have told me to strip in front of the crowd. There was one word for women who went without a bra where I grew up: 'hussy'. But however hard I tried to hide my fear, I felt like the odd one out, a teenage outsider standing on the edge of an adult party pretending to be part of it. Desperate to keep my secrets, I was mortified when a magazine ran a picture of me under the headline 'The virgin queen of pop'. It felt as if everything I was trying so hard to hide had been spelled out in black and white for the world to see.

It was a strange kind of torture. Being 'good' was who I was. It was how I'd learned to be. It was also core to my professional image and Marian knew that. Plus, we all knew what happened to girls and women who got on the wrong side of it all. In early 1967, police had raided Keith Richards' home Redlands and arrested him and Mick Jagger for drug offences. But it was Marianne Faithfull who'd been most viciously hung out to dry. I didn't know her well but felt desperate for Marianne and scared too.

It was like walking a high wire that was weighted against you: be available enough to be desirable, but not threatening; glamorous enough to be aspirational, but not alienating; know enough to play the part, but be careful not to overstep the line in the way men could.

In other words: you were damned either way.

# 20

# John Lennon Plays Me Sgt. Pepper

*John Lennon could be utterly charming one minute and slightly terrifying the next. At least that's how he felt to teenage me. While Paul and the rest of the boys were good company, kind and playful, I found John far more complicated – acerbic, mischievous and cutting even, because he was so quick-witted he left most people several steps behind. Deep down, I was as keen for John to respect me as I was for everyone else to. And it made me so anxious to fit in that I was always anticipating what to say and how, rather than just being myself and present in the moment. Always my biggest mistake.*

*However intimidating I found John, though, I loved Cyn and enjoyed going to see them at Kenwood, their house in leafy Surrey. Everyone seemed to be moving into country mansions in those days. Ringo was just down the road from John. Brian Epstein had bought a big place in Sussex. I couldn't really understand why they were all leaving London – rebelling on one hand, living near the golf club on the other. But they were older and had kids, I reasoned. Maybe that's just what happened in your twenties.*

*From the outside, Kenwood was a traditional looking house set in large gardens. But inside it was a mishmash of both their styles.*

*Cyn's mother loved antique-hunting, and tasteful pieces they'd bought were scattered around the rooms. Set against them were bits and pieces of the psychedelia John loved so much – half-finished paintings and sketches he'd drawn on the walls. It felt like a collision between the past and the future.*

*One afternoon, sometime in early 1967, I went out to Kenwood to see Cyn and we'd been chatting for a while when John came in.*

*'Wanna hear the new album?' he asked.*

*That felt like a very loaded question.*

*I felt nervous around John even on the best of days. You never knew quite what you'd get and I was always keen to play it cool, not be too chatty or needy. And that afternoon, I had no idea where he'd been the night – or morning – before and how hungover he might be, so it made me even more cautious of the danger that always seemed to surround him and was definitely part of his attraction.*

*But then again, John Lennon was also offering to play me his new album.*

*'Love to,' I said, trying to hit the perfect point between casual friend and serious artist.*

*John put on the record and I started to listen. But the more I heard, the more my insides twisted into knots. It was amazing, new. But also, what on earth was it? I had no idea. It was a new Beatles album though. I had to say something. Didn't I?*

*John wandered in and out, Cyn sipped her tea, I prayed for lightning to strike and save me from having to speak. My face felt like it was turning to rubber as I tried to say something.*

*'Amazing,' I finally stammered.*

*I don't know if John even looked at me.*

*'Do you want a biscuit?' Cyn said soothingly.*

*I ate it wordlessly, kicking myself at my stupidity. In a world of people who seemed to eat books, art and film for breakfast, there were a lot of conversations happening in those days that I felt too intimidated to join in. But I was confused by what I'd just heard: horns blaring and crowd sounds, references to marmalade skies and melody playing backwards. I just didn't know what to make of it. My mind was racing.*

*All I can say in my defence is this: I don't think I was the only one who felt that way on a first listen to* Sgt. Pepper's Lonely Hearts Club Band.

# 21

# Who Do They Want Me to Be?

As the Beatles burned ever higher into the atmosphere, I was floundering musically. In fact, I was beginning to feel increasingly frustrated with Mickie Most. The follow-up to 'The Boat That I Row' was due to be released in June 1967 while I was in America doing publicity for the film premiere of *To Sir, With Love*. The movie would be released later in the year in the UK, so it seemed obvious to me that the film theme tune should be my next single.

But Mickie was insistent. He wanted a track called 'Let's Pretend' on the A-side, a ballad with yet more Hammond organ and a lot of high notes that I didn't feel really tapped into the power of my voice. The reason 'Shout' had done well was because I connected to it, but 'Let's Pretend' didn't come close. Worse, it meant 'To Sir, With Love' would be lost on the B-side.

'He really does know best Lu,' Marian reasoned when I complained. 'Look at everything Mickie has done. We've got to listen to what he says.'

Mickie got his way and 'Let's Pretend' was released while I was in the States. It reached number eleven, which everyone was happy with, and I wasn't going to complain about charting.

But another part of me remained frustrated that 'To Sir' wasn't getting the exposure I was convinced it should have. It was a slightly different kind of song and sound. I was desperate to push the lines a bit. The Beatles had gone from 'Love Me Do' to 'Lucy in the Sky with Diamonds'. Surely the public could cope if Lulu broke the formula in some tiny way?

But, as ever, there was no time to dwell for too long. Push forwards. Busy. Busy. Acquire the next string that everyone from records to TV execs believed I should have in my bow. This time it was comedy sketches and I'd been offered a new TV show with Mike Yarwood and Ray Fell called *Three of a Kind*. I played the straight woman and, yet again, pushed myself to do my best at something I wasn't convinced I would excel at, but everyone assured me I could. Dusty had done her own TV show and soon Cilla would too. TV was a medium that other female singers were also moving into as we all just tried to keep working.

But while I knew it was a great opportunity, all I really wanted to do was make – and promote – the kind of music I was soaking in as I watched masters of their art at work. Nina Simone had appeared on stage looking like she was about to turn milk. I couldn't believe she got away with it. But when she started to sing, I realised she wasn't there to 'perform'. Nina transformed into a queen – regal, fierce, frightening even – and wasn't going to stoop to worrying about what her courtiers thought of her. Midway through, her head had snapped towards her bass player like a cobra and I recognised the look. You could almost feel the heat of Nina's white rage coming off her. She commanded him back into line with barely a glance.

I was transfixed.

Jimi Hendrix, too, at a Sunday-night gig at the Saville Theatre, the place Brian Epstein leased. It was one of his first big London gigs and everyone was there: Paul, John and Cyn, Eric and Jack Bruce. I sat next to Stevie Marriott from the Small Faces and his girlfriend Chrissie Shrimpton, Jean's sister. Jimi blew the roof off and did it all over again a few months later when he went back to the Saville and opened with 'Sgt. Pepper' days after it was released before slamming into 'Foxy Lady'.

Both Nina and Jimi were unapologetically authentic. They were pushing boundaries while I felt more and more hemmed in by mine, still too scared to go against the force of the people above me. Besides, I was doing what they needed me to do: winning awards, popular with the public, and still charting. A lot of teenage me loved it, of course. I was in magazines, friends with 'stars' and had more money than I'd ever dreamed of. But, deep down, I also knew I didn't feel comfortable musically. I wasn't growing in the way I wanted to.

The trouble is, though, it's impossible to be authentic when you don't truly know who you are yet.

# 22

# Waking up with All My Clothes On

George Harrison was playing a ukulele, Peter Tork had a banjo and Keith Moon was drumming the table. It was about 3am and, between the music and the copious amount of LSD in the room, it was one of the wildest parties I'd ever been to.

The previous night, I'd finished supporting the Monkees on three dates at Wembley in front of a crowd of 10,000. It had felt as if I was flying as I stood looking out at the sea of faces. Getting to know the boys had been fun and I was thrilled when Mike Nesmith said he loved my voice before drilling me about how I got it so husky. When Peter Tork and Micky Dolenz told me they wanted to see London, I took them to the King's Road just before the shops shut in the hope of going unnoticed, but we ended up being mobbed.

The party was being held at a club called The Speakeasy, and Brian Epstein had organised it so that the Monkees could meet the Beatles. A big crowd of us had gathered: John and Cyn, George and Pattie, Paul and Jane, plus Eric Clapton, the Who boys and other musicians. Dusty was there too and we chatted as the room filled and the music started.

'You're so brave Lu!' she said as we talked. 'So confident. Nothing ever scares you.'

'Are you serious?' I exclaimed. 'Look at your music. You're so good at getting what you want.'

Through kohl-heavy eyes, Dusty looked at me kindly.

'I don't mean all that,' she said. 'I mean how you are in yourself. You do it all. You're fearless.'

Whenever I was with Dusty, I could always sense a fragility about her. She was so vulnerable, and this was a huge part of her appeal – people could feel it in her music. She watched me carefully and was always interested in my progress.

It was a night to remember.

'If you think it's a bus, it's a bus,' I could hear Ringo Starr saying again and again. 'If you want it to be a lamp, it's a lamp.'

'Yeah man.'

'But no. I really mean it. If you think it's a bus ... '

You get the picture.

A lot of people were experimenting with drugs back then, but I never wanted to. Seeing my father lose control had made me terrified of behaving unpredictably and I wasn't sure how drugs might affect me. I never saw people take them, but could feel the room tilt as people got high, and merging with it was an increasing interest in expanding consciousness, Eastern spirituality and meditation. If I heard the words, 'You've got to go to India' once, I heard them a thousand times.

I'd never got further than Spain outside of work trips.

But with so many people talking about meditation, Pattie and Cyn took me to one of the Maharishi's people, who taught

Transcendental Meditation. I was given my personal mantra, which turned out to be the widely known primordial sound 'Om', so I felt duped, didn't engage and gave up when it failed to have an instant transformative effect.

And on nights like that one at The Speakeasy, I didn't need anything other than the feeling of being in the crowd – at the centre of a propulsive, ecstatic feeling of youth and invincibility. The music, the dancing – and a fair few drinks – were enough for me because three years after 'Shout', I still had to pinch myself I was even in the same room as the Beatles and the Stones.

Some friends tried to convince me that LSD was the key to their creativity; others said I should just push the boundaries. But I was afraid and no one pressured or made fun of me. So, if I was out and a joint started getting passed around, I'd usually get up, make my excuses and leave the grown-ups to it.

The only bit about the whole psychedelic thing I truly loved was John's Rolls-Royce Phantom V. He'd had it custom-painted in a mad swirl of flowers, Romany scrolls and zodiac signs – and always insisted a woman had screamed in outrage when she saw this desecration of Britishness drive down Piccadilly. I, however, loved the Rolls so much when we got into it on nights out that I rapidly replaced the stately Austin Princess I'd bought with an oyster pink Mini covered in decals of daisies that I'd bought in LA.

Apart from a few bells around my neck, it was the closest I ever got to a psychedelic phase.

In the hours after the crowd drifted away from The Speakeasy and the sun rose over London, I fell asleep in Peter Tork's hotel room with all my clothes on. Meanwhile, Micky Dolenz was still high on acid and infamously decided to go for a walk in Hyde Park. He ended up singing from a bandstand for a crowd of hundreds who couldn't believe their idol was out in the wilds of everyday life among them. And, years later, I remembered something Peter Tork had said during those days at Wembley when he'd described his life as a long series of closed passages that he couldn't break out of: to cars, hotel rooms, dressing rooms and stages.

I think it's this feeling of being trapped in a gilded cage – plus the money, power rush and unreality of fame – that drives so many people in the world of celebrity to get drawn into drugs. It's an escape from an existence which might seem perfect, but doesn't always feel it; a rebellion from a life in which so much is handed to you that it sometimes feels there are no limits to push.

Within a few months of The Speakeasy party, Brian had died from an overdose and I, like so many other people, was devastated. He'd invited me and Joanne, his PA, to the country that weekend, but we couldn't go, so Brian had come back to London where he died. And in the years that followed, it felt as if we lost so many great talents. Janis Joplin. Keith Moon. John Bonham. We're still losing them today.

# 23

# America Wants Lulu

The telegram was just one line: 'America wants Lulu. Please send soonest.'

I had no idea I'd step off a plane and into a whirlwind. But out of all the music I've recorded, 'To Sir, With Love' is probably the track that proves just how mercurial success can be. It had sunk without trace on the B-side of 'Let's Pretend' in the UK, but something extraordinary started to happen during the autumn of 1967. 'To Sir' entered the US Billboard charts and started to climb. And climb. Americans had taken the film to their hearts. Now they took the music too.

It was all down to radio DJs who'd got copies of 'Let's Pretend', but started flipping them to play 'To Sir'. They felt just as I did about the song. Something about it would connect. And it did. A track that had done nothing at home kept climbing. And suddenly, everyone wanted me stateside.

After listening to my mother's dreams of America as a child, New York was all I'd imagined it would be: busy streets, buildings disappearing into the clouds, yellow taxis and steam billowing up from the manhole covers. It was like stepping onto the film set I'd seen all my life on screen. But the biggest thrill? America seemed to love me as much as I loved it.

'Hey, are you that kid Lulu who's in the film with Sidney Poitier?' taxi drivers would yell.

Fans would gather in crowds outside the hotels where I stayed as I crisscrossed the country doing promotion, and every detail of America – from the food and cars to the beds and fashion – fascinated me.

'I saw a woman walking down Park Avenue with four poodles,' I'd garble on the phone to Betty. 'And they serve cottage cheese on top of fruit for breakfast. The strawberries are huge.'

'Cottage cheese for breakfast!' Betty shrieked back as if I was being served a head on a platter.

'And the beds are so big, we'd fit all of us in one. The studio even sent a big, long limousine to pick me up and take me everywhere.'

'Did you hear all that Eddie? Marie's on the phone from America. Come and speak to her.'

And my dad would come on the phone.

'I can't believe it hen,' Eddie would say. 'We can't wait to see the film. Who'd have believed it Marie?'

Then Betty would grab the phone back.

'What hair are they wearing over there? What's the fashion? Everyone's asking.'

But as transfixed as I was by burgers and breakfast options, I was soon introduced to another strange quirk of fame: the bigger your profile, the more inside the club you get. On one memorable afternoon, for instance, Billy Friedkin – who I'd been introduced to and would famously go on to direct films including *The French Connection* and *The Exorcist* – told me he was dropping in to see a friend and asked if I wanted to join. Within the hour, I found myself watching Cher hold court as she lay on a giant bed, in a giant house, as lean and lithe as you'd imagine and more comfortable in her own skin than I'd ever seen a woman be.

'Don't be so fucking stupid,' she said with a laugh to some guy who was trying to impress her.

On another night, I was invited to a party held on the crowded deck of a luxury yacht and my eyes were out on sticks as Warren Beatty wandered past, closely followed by Roman Polanski and Sharon Tate. The only word I can find to describe her beauty is 'translucent'. She literally seemed to shine.

My most memorable meeting, however, came when 'To Sir' hit number one on the Billboard charts and I flew back over for twenty-four hours to appear on *The Ed Sullivan Show* before returning weeks later to do *The Tonight Show* with Johnny Carson and *The Joey Bishop Show*. Ray Charles was performing at a club called The Copacabana and I could hardly breathe as I sat in the audience listening to the artist who, for me, embodied pure genius. When I was invited backstage afterwards, I just about mumbled something to my all-time hero.

Back home, speculation mounted in the British press that I was going to make a move to the US as I got an American agent and Marian started fielding big offers. But while she'd always said Americans would love me, she suddenly seemed to cool on the idea.

'I'm not sure Lu,' she'd say as we talked. 'Look how homesick you were when you left Scotland.

'And the new series of *Three of a Kind* is doing well. The BBC is talking about your own show. You'll be the star. Let's not make any moves right now. You're doing so well. And you're only nineteen. There's still so much time.'

'But it's America. We've got to try. Haven't we?'

'And what would I do with Gerald and the children?' Marian continued. 'I can't just move us all over there. Do you see?'

Of course, I understand why Marian made the decisions she did. She was a wife and mother, as well as my manager. And life is always going to be a series of missed moments. You'll always look back and wonder. But when I think about that period now, it's not the possibility of a career in the States that nags at me. So many people are eaten up there and I might have been too. But the missed opportunity for my music in the UK with 'To Sir' is something I've always wondered about.

It stayed at number one for five weeks, sold more than a million copies and became the biggest-selling single in the US of 1967. Could it have done the same at home? Just the flip of a disc might have taken my music career in a whole new direction if it had been put on the A-side in the UK. Because hits create opportunities and 'To Sir' was a different kind of song that might have changed how the public saw me and allowed me to start making the kind of music I really believed in. But more and more back then, I was letting myself get pushed in so many directions, I had started to lose sight of what really mattered.

## 24

# Saturday Night Prime Time

Television was very seductive. At least it was to my manager. And I let myself get distracted because singing meant being away from home, draughty venues and long nights. Most of all, performing alone had made me feel more and more lonely professionally since splitting with the Luvvers. Of course, I had musicians who I worked with regularly, and they were great talents. But it's not the same as being part of a group with an equal stake in a shared career. Ultimately, you go on stage alone as a solo artist.

Television, though, was a break from all that – plus, hair and make-up, a musical director, set designer, orchestra and your own bed at the end of the night. With ten years of professional singing under my belt, I was ready for some comfort.

It was a mistake.

Mickie and I carried on recording and I was pleased when he agreed to try something a bit different. 'Love Loves to Love Love' was a track that drummers loved because it was technically challenging and I liked it too. But when it charted low at number thirty-two, I assume Mickie got nervous and we returned to a more familiar formula with 'Me, the Peaceful Heart'. Back up to number nine. I thought the song was okay. But not fire. And while I managed to convince Mickie to put 'Morning Dew' by Bonnie Dobson and Tim Rose and the Bee Gees' 'To Love Somebody' on my first album, he chose the singles. As far as the execs were concerned, Mickie was a master of his game. What more proof did I need? The singles were creating hits for EMI.

Marian could see I was frustrated and I think that's why she was so delighted when the BBC approached us. Aged just nineteen, they wanted me to be the face of my own TV show. *Lulu's Back in Town* would air on Tuesday nights, a pre-recorded variety show with guests like Georgie Fame and the Everly Brothers. I'd sing, present and, most of all, be the face of a prestigious show.

'Are you serious?' Betty had screeched when I told her the news. 'Your own television programme Marie! Are you not a bit young hen?'

I certainly felt daunted by the idea. In all my previous TV work, I'd presented alongside other people or been the foil to comedians. This was another challenge.

'You'll handle this like you do everything else,' Marian insisted. 'This is a huge opportunity for you. And I know you can do it. You're a natural on the screen.

'The BBC wouldn't offer you something like this if they didn't think you could do it. And it's a chance for us to broaden things out, not just rely on music. We never know what will happen with it. This will give you options.'

I agreed, prepared, as ever, to throw myself in, learn on the job and keep smiling my way through the nerves. The series would also give me the chance to promote my music and, midway through it, my next single 'Boy' was released and got to number fifteen – a reasonable result. The Mickie singles also had good traction, staying on the chart for two to three months each time, so the execs were pleased. Marian too. Between the records and my own TV show, I was still riding high.

The BBC show was a huge learning curve, but I enjoyed the challenge compared to how lightweight, almost soulless, my music was beginning to feel. Mickie was making the right choices as a producer, but he was the man who'd created the Animals and that was the kind of material I loved. What we were doing felt more like the novelty tunes of his other hit act, Herman's Hermits. I understood Mickie had a hard choice to make. There was a chasm increasingly opening up in the industry between 'cool' and 'not cool'. It was going to be hard to flip Little Miss Sunshine into cutting-edge singer. But when Mickie announced his next single choice, I decided I'd had enough.

'Are you kidding me?' I exploded at Marian. 'It's dreadful. Why isn't he finding me something more powerful? Something with an edge? Material that really suits my voice?'

'I understand Lu,' Marian insisted. 'But this is the best we can do for now. Mickie's got the formula right.

'And we have to think long term. The more successful you are, the more powerful you are and then we get to call the shots. But for now, let's do what Mickie advises.'

I resigned myself to their plan.

The new song was called 'I'm a Tiger' and it sounded to me like a nursery rhyme. Great pop is an art and I was never going to be a snob about it. But now I was being sent back to childhood and stripped of the power of my vocal abilities – the very thing people had connected to since I was a kid. Day after day, I'd tussle with Mickie about what we were doing, where I was going, as he insisted he knew best and I pleaded with him for a different direction. He wouldn't listen to a word I said though.

'What about writing your own material?' Marian would suggest occasionally.

At that point, I didn't even know how to start and the fear made me shut it down.

'I can't,' I'd cry. 'I've never even had a piano lesson. I haven't got a clue.'

Songwriting felt completely overwhelming to me, tapping into the insecurity I felt about how much education I had missed, the musical training I'd never had and the lack of confidence I felt about my work, however much I faked a breezy attitude. Even with all the success I'd had, I still ran off stage when my audience started to applaud, subconsciously feeling unworthy.

Today, the industry has changed so much and most artists now are singer-songwriters. But back then, it was different. Some women like Janis Joplin and Joni Mitchell wrote material, of course, but many others either didn't or only the odd song. The kindest torture Marian could have inflicted on me would have been to book studio time, preferably on a tiny island in the middle of a large ocean, and leave me marooned there until I got something on paper, but she didn't. She would never have pushed me like that because Marian didn't think that way. And she listened to the industry bosses who said I was doing exactly what I should be.

But my unhappiness about the music meant I found it harder and harder to sleep as I pushed it all down while feeling more and more lost. When 'I'm a Tiger' got to number nine, Mickie was the hitmaker once again. But unease kept growing inside me. It felt more and more like an impossible choice: commercial success or doing something I believed in.

I could see Mickie's logic: we'd tried something different with 'Love Loves to Love Love' and the public hadn't connected to it. I was trapped by the industry – their idea of who I was and the music they wanted from me. I was a young, teenage star. Keep it light. Keep it bright.

All this, I suppose, is why TV felt like a lifeline I clutched on to. My music didn't feel dependable and I had to keep looking after my family. I'd done it practically as a child and had now taken on financial commitments to them as soon as I could afford to. It was yet another way I tried to look after them and make things better. So, at least by doing TV, I'd be able to keep earning. My family's lifestyle had improved just as mine had; I couldn't take them back to notes stuffed under the lino plus the odd trip to the pawn shop because I wasn't feeling artistically satisfied. I had responsibilities, and TV would allow me to honour them.

Somewhere, deep inside me too, my mother's voice echoed: 'It doesn't cost you anything to smile Marie,' Betty would say. 'That face of yours will freeze if you don't cheer up.'

# 25

# Up a Drainpipe with Jim Morrison and Warren Beatty

*I watched drunkenly as Warren Beatty and Jim Morrison tried to climb a drainpipe on the wall of a Mayfair townhouse. We'd been having Sunday lunch at Warren's flat in South Audley Street, a large group of us gathering to eat a bit and drink even more as the smoke from what felt like a thousand joints filled the room and I prayed for fresh air.*

*I couldn't take my eyes off Warren and Jim that afternoon. They weren't just relaxed. They had the air of gods about them, the kind of supreme confidence I'd never really seen so closely before. British stars were often almost apologetic about it all, anxious not to be seen as too cocksure or arrogant. But these two didn't seem weighed down by that. Warren and his beauty. Jim, long, languid and completely at ease. And, of course, they were incredibly stoned, which helps anyone relax.*

*During those long, hazy hours when the afternoon started to slip towards evening, a fire alarm started going off, its harsh sound breaking the spell we were in.*

*'Can't we just shut it down?' someone said, annoyed at the disruption.*

*People got to their feet and walked unsteadily down into the street, glasses in hand, laughing at the adventure. And, as a small crowd of us gathered underneath the screeching alarm, wondering what to do with it, Jim and Warren looked at each other before walking up to the drainpipe and starting to climb towards the sound.*

*'Make it stop!' someone yelled.*

*'Shut the fucking thing off,' another voice cried.*

*I watched in amazement as Warren and Jim climbed upwards. They couldn't just wreck a fire alarm. Didn't they realise they might get arrested? That someone would see them and call the police? But standing on that pavement staring upwards, I realised: they were beyond the realms of ordinary life, so immersed in the gigantic vistas of American fame, the rules didn't apply. These men were completely free.*

IV

# 26

# Falling for a Bee Gee

'He seems a bit young,' I said to my friend Joanne as we stood in the BBC bar.

'But he's lovely Lu!' she replied. 'Give him a chance. I think he likes you.'

I looked at the small bearded man standing with his brothers and wondered. He looked gentle, kind, and I'd never been interested in bad boys. I liked men who made me feel safe.

A group of us had just recorded the Boxing Day edition of *Top of the Pops*. The Monkees, the Stones and Long John Baldry had played – or rather mimed – I'd performed with a head of curls, and the Bee Gees, who'd been taken on by Cream manager Robert Stigwood, had done their first UK number one, 'Massachusetts'. Barry, Robin and Maurice: three brothers whose musicality and harmonies were getting them noticed.

As I stood chatting with Joanne, Maurice bounded up to talk. Face like an open book: wide smile, brown eyes, a suit with a polo neck. Clean-cut.

'He thought you were great,' Joanna told me on the phone a few days later. 'I saw him at Robert's office and he's just too shy to say it to your face.'

But although Maurice and I went on a few dates, I was half-hearted about it. That didn't stop the press, of course. They went wild whenever I even sniffed in the direction of someone with a profile and my 'romance' with Maurice quickly got into the papers. Thanks, I suspected, to Robert Stigwood, playing it up in order to keep his act in the headlines. More column inches were created by some dates with Davy Jones – who I was convinced I was falling in love with after dating him briefly when I was performing in the US before finding out he had a pregnant girlfriend – and a few nights out with George Best. The pop star and the Bee Gee. The pop star and the Monkee. The pop star and the star footballer.

If anyone believed the headlines, I was heavily committed to all three.

I wasn't.

'Never marry a wee man like your father,' was the only comment Betty made on it all. 'They always have a chip on their shoulder.'

In truth, the most serious relationship I had was with my diary, where I wrote page after page of teenage angst about my dates – who I preferred, why I'd gone off them and how heartbroken I felt.

After a three-week stint at The Talk of The Town in February 1968, a big cabaret venue where artists including Eartha Kitt, Shirley Bassey and Judy Garland had played, I flew to America for a month at The Coconut Grove in Los Angeles. But when I bumped into Maurice again back in London, something finally clicked. He was easy company, funny, generous and gave me so much attention that it was intoxicating.

Plus, there was his talent. Maurice was a skilled bassist, pianist and songwriter with a voice which seamlessly flipped into the falsetto that would become such a key part of the Bee Gees' distinctive harmonies. It was fascinating for me as a solo singer to hear them, and the more time I spent with Maurice, the more I was drawn to the musicality he shared so powerfully with his brothers. Plus, they had working-class roots and came from Manchester, so I felt at home with their humour, values and camaraderie. They'd also started out in music young. Their father, Hughie, was a drummer in a big band when he met their mother, Barbara, who was a singer. I loved them both and the boys had always financially supported their family, so we shared that too.

Barry, the typical older brother, was the leader of the pack, the diamond at the centre of the wheel. Robin was lightening quick and constantly vying with Barry to be leader. And Maurice completed the circle with his easy, gentle nature. But, like most siblings, the three often fell out, made up and fell out all over again.

Maurice and I started spending more time with Barry and his wife Linda. It was easy, fun and filled with music. Craving the kind of magic the brothers shared professionally, and the family feeling they quickly wrapped me in, I rapidly fell in love with Maurice because I was longing for true companionship – that feeling of opening the door at home to find your person sitting there. I was tired of being alone in a world of couples and I think part of me also wanted to create a feeling of family. Maurice also understood the downsides of a life that is made to feel perfect and aspirational from the outside, but creates a certain distance between you and many other people too. Being with him quietened all those feelings and he swept me up, which is why, just a year after we seriously started dating, we decided to get married.

'You're making a mistake,' Billy told me.

I'd moved my brother down to London when he was sixteen, keen for him to leave Glasgow – the gangs, the violence and increasing tension with Eddie – because as Billy had grown up, he'd found it harder to keep his tongue held about my father's behaviour. After going to drama school and deciding it wasn't for him, Billy had started to carve out a career in music and was doing well. He was talented, hungry, hard-working, and he and Maurice were close friends. The two of them had even started writing music together – but all this didn't mean Billy was convinced about us getting married.

'None of your business,' I hissed.

Billy laughed as he looked at me with his shrewd, intelligent eyes.

'I love Mo, but he's a baby,' he said. 'He'll never be able to keep up with you.'

Thankfully, Betty and Eddie were all for it. They were about the same age as us when they married, and they liked Mo and his family. Never that comfortable with the starry set and fame, they also appreciated that Mo came from a tribe like ours. Barry, however, was even more against the idea than Billy and I was crushed when he was quoted in a newspaper saying that we were too young.

'What does he know?' I spat at Maurice. 'And how can he do that to us?'

'Just ignore it Lu. He always wants to be in charge. But it's our life. We know what we're doing.'

The more people questioned our decision, the more protective I felt of our relationship. People had been telling me what to do for so long and I wasn't a kid anymore. I wanted to share my life. And Maurice was the person I wanted to do that with.

# 27

# Jimi Hendrix vs. Auntie BBC

Stanley Dorfman was a cutting-edge TV director and producer and I couldn't wait to work with him. After creating *Top of the Pops* and Dusty's solo show for the BBC, he was working on my next solo TV series, *Happening for Lulu*.

Still continually in and out of the newspapers and magazines, doing TV adverts, touring, releasing music and now another TV show, I was so ever-present that a comic in the US had even parodied me with a sketch which went along the lines of:

'And today in London, pop star Lulu went to the hairdresser.

'And then pop star Lulu went to a restaurant.

'And then pop star Lulu won an award.'

But Marian insisted keeping my profile high would only open up new opportunities, and this new solo show was going to be a step up from my previous TV work because it was live and would be broadcast on Saturday, the biggest day of the week for BBC1.

'This is huge Lu,' Marian told me. 'The kind of work that will give you longevity. A whole new direction.'

What appealed to me most, though, was that Stanley wanted to go beyond the standard variety format to mix well-known musicians with up-and-coming talent to give the show a more cutting-edge feel. Ironically, TV was giving me the chance to go in a more contemporary direction that music wasn't offering.

'It's going to be forty-five minutes of live, unscripted, anything-can-happen television,' Stanley said.

Little did he know.

Maurice and I sang together on the launch episode, but things ramped up for the second because the Jimi Hendrix Experience had been booked as star guests. They were flying in to start a UK tour and it was a massive coup to have them on. I liked Jimi a lot and had met him out and about at awards shows. He had a gentle manner and was so polite, far removed from so many of the brash music execs I knew. And I was excited to have him on because it was an odd mix, and playing against type was what Stanley wanted to do. I was also keen to challenge the perception of me as the always-good girl next door.

The day of Jimi's performance started out regularly enough. He arrived with the band as I was rehearsing, so I didn't see them when they disappeared into a dressing room where they apparently lit a joint. Cut to about 5.50pm and the nation was settled in front of their TVs as the well and truly stoned members of the Jimi Hendrix Experience did 'Voodoo Child'. Then the camera panned to me: bright-eyed, smiling and very unstoned.

'They're gonna sing for you now the song that absolutely made them in this country,' I said as I looked into the camera lens. 'And I'd love to hear them sing it: "Hey Joe".'

Jimi, however, decided to jettison the plan about a minute into 'Hey Joe'.

'We'd like to stop playing this rubbish,' he suddenly said. 'And dedicate a song to the Cream, regardless of what kind of group they might be in. We dedicate this to Eric Clapton, Ginger Baker and Jack Bruce.'

Jimi was clearly feeling emotional. News had just broken that Cream had split. But as he and the band launched into an off-script version of 'Sunshine of Your Love', I saw confusion and then horror wash over the floor manager's face. We were live. Everything was tightly timed. Jimi was going rogue.

It was certainly anything-can-happen TV.

The poor floor manager looked as if he was about to faint, going increasingly purple in the face, frantically making slashing motions at his throat to get the band to cut. The 6 o'clock news was going to be late. Jimi Hendrix had taken Auntie captive.

Not that he cared. Jimi took no notice of all the frantic attempts to get him to stop playing. In fact, he seemed to be really enjoying himself.

'We're being put off the air,' he said with a smile before slowing the music down and drawing out the last few chords for what felt like hours.

The cameras cut. The floor manager almost combusted. And presumably Stanley did too.

Later on, as I went back to my dressing room, Jimi walked towards me.

'Lu,' he said. 'I'm sorry if I ... '

I looked at him. Jimi smiled, a schoolboy who'd got one over on a teacher.

'Not a problem Jimi, you're the best,' I said as I ran to change into the next costume.

The papers screamed. BBC management melted down and announced they would be banning Jimi from all TV and radio channels to teach him a lesson. It only made him more famous and more interesting. But I presume the Jimi Hendrix Experience spooked the BBC bosses so much they dared not take any more risks because the series was hastily reworked and given a new title: *Lulu*. No more anything-can-happen. Instead, the new-look show was going to catapult me back into another more reliable format – one that was known by millions because of its well-honed and predictable formula. Over the next few weeks, I'd be singing a selection of songs before a public vote.

I was entering *Eurovision*.

# 28

# Winning *Eurovision*

J ust under five years separated the release of 'Shout' and me standing on stage in Madrid for *Eurovision* 1969. And if 'Shout' was the moment I first got swept up in the whirlwind, *Eurovision* was the point at which I felt so far above the ground, I didn't know how I'd ever land again. It had been five years of constant work and performing as Marian took me into different areas of music and entertainment to try to extend my career beyond the usual short path of pop princesses. Now, I was being given the chance to perform on pop music's largest platform – on a show that reached millions – and while Marian had told me that it was a great opportunity to extend my profile, it also felt like a lie.

Singing all the possible *Eurovision* songs each week on my BBC show as the public voted for their favourite only strengthened that feeling. The tracks ran the gamut of Euro eccentricity – from pop with a marching band to pop with the odd, and very Greek, addition of a bouzouki. It was less feeding my soul, more sucking it out through my eyeballs. There are many worse jobs than doing a primetime TV show, but, artistically, it felt far away from the passion that had started me out in music when I'd connected to songs that made me feel a certain way, spoke to the confusion inside me and made me feel safe in the chaos of home. First, my recording career had gone in a direction I didn't feel comfortable with. Now, *Eurovision*, with its manufactured pop and frothy tunes, felt like the apex of that drift.

I did, of course, understand Marian's logic about why I should do it.

'It will be huge exposure,' she said. 'Singing *Eurovision* entries will push the ratings up on the BBC, which means you'll get the pick of bigger projects next time. And, you'll be seen all over Europe. Who knows where it might lead?'

Marian was a shrewd operator when it came to the commercial aspects of the entertainment industry and had links to many of its biggest players. The right-hand side of my brain understood her point, but the left side was panicking.

'I want to change things up and this feels like more of the same,' I said as she kept encouraging me.

'Think of where it might take you Lu,' she said. 'You're still so young. And the world will be your oyster. We can't pass up a chance like this. Don't change the formula too much now. We don't know what might happen and this is guaranteed exposure.'

Marian was right in some ways, of course. It was a huge honour to be asked to represent the UK and I had to respect the responsibility I'd been given. But while *Eurovision* was a great showcase if you wanted to establish a career, I already had one and wasn't sure the competition would help my music get to where I wanted it to be. But did I put my foot down and make Marian see my side of the story?

No.

It would take me years to learn how to say that word and, at just twenty, I didn't even know what change might look like for my music because I hadn't had a chance to consider it. Nor did I have the language to explain what I wanted or how I felt. I had yet to even start to get to know myself so, as ever, I went along with the plans feeling sharply divided between excitement and dread. The wheels were in motion, plans made and I had to turn up, sing and do as I was told.

I performed all the potential tracks on the BBC backed by Johnny Harris and his orchestra, and we laid bets at the start on which song would win. It was practically unanimous. We knew it would be 'Boom Bang-a-Bang' because you didn't need to understand the sentiment of the words, and the chorus wormed into your brain – perfect *Eurovision* material.

It's hard to talk negatively about a song that is loved by so many. Now I can feel affection for 'Boom Bang-a-Bang' because it's a piece of our shared cultural furniture, the kind of song everyone knows. And how many pop tunes out of the millions that have been released have that kind of staying power? But back then? Another nursery rhyme. Another childlike confection. With a Euro twist.

I was also terrified of being humiliated in front of millions. There was no guarantee of success. The voting seemed to be hugely political. And while Sandie Shaw had won in 1967 for the United Kingdom, I might well flop. Who knew if the Eurozone wanted more fluffy pop this year? Would they plump for a more sophisticated Italian ballad or something else this time?

Betty and Eddie were so excited. I took them with me to Madrid along with Maurice's mother Barbara. But I felt overwhelmed and exhausted by the time we got there. Everything had been moving so fast, for so long, that I could hardly make sense of it. At night, I'd take the edges off with a few drinks with my family to come down from the high of performing. Then, the next day, again: turn up, do as you're told, throw yourself into whatever you're asked to do.

The question I've often been asked since then is how did I survive starting out when I was so young? Luck played a part. As did Marian's protection. But underneath all that was anxiety, which made me a desperate people-pleaser who always wanted to do my best. Then there was my innate optimistic streak that tried to make the best of whatever was handed to me. Put it all together and I look back at the girl who appeared on the *Eurovision* stage as a puppet, tugged into the latest shape that was asked of her.

'Boom Bang-a-Bang' wasn't my favourite song, but I told myself I had to be grateful to be given this chance and perform the song as well as I could, so I certainly didn't walk on stage with a head filled with negative thoughts. I got on with it and gave it my absolute all. But even the outfit I performed in that night was part of the fiction which had been woven around me: a bubble pink chiffon minidress covered in appliqued white flowers – the perfect doll outfit to go with such a lightweight song.

With sixteen countries competing, I risked looking like a complete fool if I came last, so I sung my heart out. Then, as now, I admire the bravery of anyone who's prepared to put themselves out there and enter. You can laugh at *Eurovision*, you can joke about the music, but you have to be courageous – or slightly deranged – to put yourself in such a massive spotlight. Most failure is quiet. *Eurovision* is not.

So, on the night, I gave it my all and delivered. Walking off stage, I sat down with the other performers to wait for the marks to be given, veering between not daring to look at anyone who got 'nul points', because I felt bad that they had to smile through the pain, and smiling maniacally myself when I was marked high – desperate to do well but my mind also in a daze.

'Boom Bang-a-Bang' pulled ahead early. Relief. Then dropped back. Anxiety. Spain, the Netherlands and France started going up the table before the UK was awarded more points. After what felt like hours of voting, it all came down to the final marks from Finland. Spain, the Netherlands and France were on eighteen. The UK had seventeen. Finland announced their points. Three to Ireland and Sweden. Two to Switzerland. One to Italy.

There was still just one point between the United Kingdom and the top three with the final mark to go.

'United Kingdom,' a voice said. 'One point.'

The place erupted. I smiled like a Stepford wife. For the first time in *Eurovision* history, four acts had tied for first place and I was one of them. Euphoria tinged with disbelief. I went back on stage, sang again, feeling strangely distant from it all, and looked at the beaming smiles of my parents. It took years to feel enough humour and affection to perform 'Boom Bang-a-Bang' again on

stage. I think the memories associated with it were just too difficult for a long time.

The worst thing though?

I'd just married Maurice and, while I had swung far away
from the music I wanted to do, my husband and his brothers
were establishing a career that was so authentically them, and
true to their talent, they'd make musical history.

# 29

# Lulu and Maurice Get Hitched

During all those years of writing romantic angst in my diary and dreaming of my wedding day, I hadn't expected thousands of fans, news headlines and the very real fear of being crushed to death before reaching the church.

The service was held in Gerrard's Cross because Maurice's parents lived nearby, and we'd hoped to keep it quiet and small. But as Eddie and I arrived in a vintage white Rolls-Royce the Bee Gees had bought, there were people lining the roads with just a few policemen trying to hold them back. We could hardly get the car door open as I pleaded with the crowd to let us out.

I kept smiling, trying not to look panicked. The people were one thing. Trying to stop my dress from being ruined was another. I was wearing a beautiful white mini topped with a floor-length fur-trimmed hooded coat, and Eddie and I had to inch towards the church door as photographers snapped pictures. After finally getting in, I discovered there was one guest who had yet to arrive – our best man, Barry Gibb. I was so relieved when he finally appeared.

It was a very small wedding with just our family and close friends. Cyn was there. Edwina and Gordon, as well as ten-year-old Andy Gibb and Maurice's niece Berry, all dressed in kilts, tartan trousers and velvet jackets ready to follow me and Dad down the aisle. Their eyes were like saucers as we made it through the doors and then Eddie's had filled with tears.

'I'm right beside you hen,' he said to me.

The stardom and the madness never mattered to my father. I was his girl and he was delighted I'd found someone who believed I was the beginning and end of his world. Once the ceremony had ended and we stood outside the church posing for pictures, I felt happier than I'd ever felt. I couldn't wait to be Mrs Gibb and start my new life. Independent. In charge of whatever direction I wanted to take. Who was I kidding?

We had lunch at the famous Le Gavroche for our families, but I was back at work the next day. We eventually squeezed in a honeymoon in Acapulco, but it didn't take long after we got back home to London for me to realise that being a wife wasn't going to be quite as perfect as I'd imagined it would be. What had I expected? I was only twenty and Maurice just nineteen. Just like my parents when they got married, we were only kids. And soon, there was another issue. I was still a virgin – and it was fast becoming the elephant in the room with me and Maurice because my worry about having sex had exploded from anxiety into full-blown fear.

I wanted to be intimate with my husband, I really did, but I was also terrified I might be physically hurt. All I knew was that something 'broke' when you first had sex and it scared me terribly. It wasn't logical. But that's how my mind unravelled all the feelings I still carried from childhood. I didn't sit down with

Maurice and spell them out, of course. Nor did he question me closely. What teenage husband is going to want to deep dive into his wife's complicated emotions? Maurice knew bits and pieces about my childhood that had slipped out in conversation, or the odd thing that Billy and I said, but he was young and I never talked to anyone about my home life as a child.

Maurice was endlessly kind, gentle and patient. He didn't push me or get angry. But I felt confused. Embarrassed. Acutely aware of what our life looked like from the outside and how different it really was. I had it all. So why was I so scared?

Maybe I wasn't the only young woman who felt afraid as the world of our Fifties childhoods sped up in the freedom of the Sixties. But I also understand now that my childhood had left me so anxious of myself, defensive and riddled with feelings I'd buried deep, that I couldn't let my guard down. And while my father's drinking was part of the story, it wasn't the whole truth.

# 30

# Ma Daddy Nearly Killed Ma Mammy

It was a cold winter's night a couple of years before I was signed to Decca. I was about thirteen and Billy and I had picked up three-year-old Edwina and baby Gordon, carrying them out of the flat with Betty following behind, eye bleeding and jaw already beginning to bruise. Running down the street, we'd stopped outside a greengrocer. Breath ragged, hearts hammering. It was dark and there was snow on the ground. I can still remember worrying about Billy's feet because he was only wearing socks.

'I've got to get them Mammy,' I said breathlessly, staring up at Betty, wanting my mother to give me permission, knowing she never would.

Running up the street, I found two policemen standing on the pavement.

'Please come,' I said in a rush. 'It's ma dad. He's nearly killed ma mammy.'

Turning around, I started running back down the street as the officers followed me.

'She's on the corner,' I called. 'With my brothers and sister. My dad's upstairs. Number nine. Soho Street.'

We watched silently as the policemen went into our building and dragged Eddie outside towards one of the red police boxes that were dotted around Glasgow. I felt sick. We all knew what happened inside those boxes, what the police did. No man wanted to be taken into one alone with Glasgow police. The wind bit through my coat as we waited until the door finally opened and Dad was led back out – ashen, bloody and frightened.

'You'll get no more trouble out of him,' a policeman said to my mother. 'He's going to sleep it off.'

Guilt filled me. Betty stared blankly. She knew this wouldn't be the end of it. We all did.

It never was.

That was the only time I ever asked for help when I was a child, and I only did so that night because I was convinced Betty would be killed. Otherwise, there was one unspoken rule in our home: don't let strangers into our business. However bad my father's violence got, we had to keep the secret.

Even now, my cheeks still burn when I think about that night. And all the others. Because while many childhood memories are worn away like rocks on a beach to grit and meaningless gravel, others can never be washed away. And it's painful to reach back into them now.

But I've skated over this topic for so long that it's time to finally tell the whole truth. So many of the choices I made during my career, as well as personal situations like my fear of intimacy with Maurice, were driven by fear that was fused into my bones as a child. It was a part of me that drove so much: the constant working, never taking a moment to breathe, scared. Always the good girl. Pushing forwards, trying to make myself feel safe.

This is what you learn as a child born into a family where drink and violence are constant undercurrents. You never fully trust. You constantly watch, strategise and read rooms in an instant, guard up, ready to fight if needed; malleable enough to bend to whatever mood is in the air. You become hypervigilant.

Guilt fills me now telling the truth about my father because I loved him very much. Eddie was a good, kind man when he was sober, and he was incredibly funny too. He cooked for us and worried about what we ate, he loved to read and was always the first one to change a nappy because Betty couldn't stand the smell. He'd come home from work in the mornings to bring Mum hot rolls in bed. And Eddie would tell her again and again that she was the most beautiful girl to ever walk the Gallowgate.

But one drink too many and Eddie would turn. Jekyll and Hyde – just like his father. Eddie Snr wasn't just a drunk though, he was also violent. The reason he lived in a Salvation Army hostel was because my father, aged about fourteen, had kicked him out of the house after Eddie Snr threw boiling water at his wife. Knowing that history can repeat itself, and with my father constantly picking on my brother, this is why I'd wanted Billy in London with me.

The violence was one thing. The fear of it, though, was almost worse – wondering what each day would bring; listening out for my father climbing the stairs after leaving the pub; watching Betty's hackles rise as he walked in; waiting for her to start quietly goading and him to erupt, even though I'd begged her not to.

'You know when Daddy comes back, don't say anything,' I'd plead with my mother. 'Don't start. Then he'll just go to bed.'

But even though she knew what would happen, Betty just couldn't seem to stop herself.

'I see you're drunk again,' she'd spit at him. 'You should be ashamed Eddie Lawrie. Wasting all that money. On whisky. What about the weans?'

'Shut the fuck up,' Dad would snarl as he lurched towards the bedroom, keen to sleep off his drinking.

But Betty wouldn't stop. Couldn't. I'd never make excuses for what my father did. There is no justification. But it was as if my parents were bound together in some terrible dance. Betty would push and goad, my father would retaliate, then she'd fly back at him, trying to give as good as she got. There was violence on both sides, but he always got the better of her. It was as if they were both so driven by their pain, they couldn't stop themselves. My mother, one part defiant, another terrified. My father, filled with rage and shame.

On good days, we'd see it coming. If my parents had been out drinking, for instance, and started to argue on the way home, my mother would run into the flat and rush us into the back bedroom before pushing a chest of drawers against the door.

'Get away from us you short-arsed bastard,' she'd shout when Eddie started hammering on the door. 'You don't deserve a family.'

The screaming. The curses. My mother putting all her body weight against the chest of drawers as she tried to keep the door closed. Eddie had turned. His rage streaming through the door towards us. Billy crying. Me pleading with my parents to stop. Just stop.

Sometimes, though, we didn't get to the back room fast enough and the physical fighting would start as my mother tried to defend herself as my father lashed out. To a child, it felt like life and death, and I was wound like a spring, finding it hard to fall asleep, having awful nightmares when I finally did and sleeping so lightly, I could have heard an eyelash drop. That's why I was too tired to concentrate at school and thoughts of home preoccupied me when I did get there. Would Dad get back early from the pub today? Would Mammy start on him? I worried all day, strategised about how to defuse the spark before it exploded that night and how I'd protect Billy, and, later on, Edwina and Gordon too, because I needed to, but also to help me feel in control.

Our story was far from unique. Violence was all around. And so much was tacitly accepted as a sad but inevitable fact of life.

'I can see your Jimmy was drunk this weekend Lizzie,' a neighbour might say as she stood on the street catching up with a friend who had a fresh black eye or split lip.

'Couldn't get the bastard off me,' Lizzie would reply with a sigh before the pair started chatting about the weather or the price of fish.

Neither of my parents ever spoke a word to us about what happened in our home or that night with the police. They slipped back into the same old ways without a word. And we as children followed their lead.

For me, it meant scurrying ashamedly the next day past neighbours who lived on the other side of our paper-thin walls. Nodding along as Mum told whoever asked about her black eye that a broom handle had accidentally hit her. Noticing the knowing looks even as people commiserated about the unpredictability of innocent household tools. I learned from the beginning to perform the role of a child smiling brightly beside a mother who wouldn't breathe a word of her shame. And I learned by example to do the same.

My dad never touched us. Not on purpose anyway. After I'd left home, he'd gone to hit Betty who was holding Edwina and had accidentally struck my sister who was knocked out. An ambulance got called and the neighbours talked to journalists, but Leslie Perrin had buried the story. Like I said, he was the master of making scandal disappear. And the only time I can remember Eddie giving me a dangerous look, I'd flown at him, heart beating in fear.

'Don't even think about it,' I'd growled. 'You just try it and I'll go straight to the police.'

Eddie had backed down, but my anger made my insides feel like a washing machine that never stopped spinning. Anger that my mother couldn't seem to shut her mouth even for our sakes. Anger that my father would hurt her before waking up sober and weak in his shame. But I learned to hide my feelings. No need for anyone else firing off into the combustible mix, and my emotions felt too out of control, too unpredictable, to let out into the open. There was no room for me to have feelings and no one to ask for help.

Making music was the one place where I could both plunge into a different part of myself and unfold my emotions just a bit. That's why it meant so much to me. And even as a tiny girl, I knew performing gave me a sense of connection and a feeling of safety that was missing at home. I could feel it as I performed and an audience, however small, responded. I loved the feeling of giving and receiving, as well as the chance to express myself. The irony that I made my name with a song called 'Shout' has not been lost on me. A song that brought my emotions out into the open, even as I hid them in plain sight. There's a reason I was so sparky and defiant on stage as a kid, but so compliant with the execs: I had learned to be all of this in my own home. Fight one moment, freeze the next.

For so many years after 'Shout', I tried to encourage Mum to leave. I wanted her to be safe. I told her again and again that I could look after her financially if she ended the marriage.

'It's not that easy with the kids,' Betty would reply with a sigh.

I didn't understand it then, but I do now. My parents were both damaged by their complicated childhoods and couldn't be without each other. They loved – and hated – each other equally. And however much I believed I'd escaped it all when I married Maurice, I learned that ghosts don't disappear. They travel with you. And my fear of intimacy was both rooted in the messages my mother had given me about it, as well as the way it had got intertwined with the violence in our home.

'You'll never get near me again,' Betty would scream at Eddie. 'You'll never put your stinking hands on me.'

Or she'd taunt him about the women she believed he was sleeping with, the pathetic nature of his sexual needs. The message was clear: men enjoyed sex, women endured it; sex created children in fragile and often violent lives; sex was secret, shameful, and Betty had to protect me from it.

And so I shut down, riddled with fear, even with the man I loved.

# 31

# Taking the Reins

It took months for me to finally overcome my fear of intimacy. But, gradually, I learned to relax with Maurice because I felt not just loved by him, but also safe. And that kind of light gradually seeps into even the darkest corners.

There were also other things happening that distracted me from dwelling too much. 'Boom Bang-a-Bang', for instance, reached number two – my biggest UK hit to date – and also charted across Europe. I didn't love the song, but a huge hit is always going to keep you busy. And then there was the money, glamour and fun of my early married life to Maurice.

After a few months in his bachelor mews home, we moved to Woodley, an eight-bedroom red-brick house I'd bought and renovated in Hampstead. I quickly threw myself into being a wife and running our – very large and very shoppable for – house. Using all the lessons I'd learned from Marian, years of watching how she did things, what she bought and how it was all presented, I poured money into Woodley to create a beautiful home that I decorated to within an inch of its life.

There was a huge kitchen where I cooked Sunday roasts, a cinema room for movie nights with friends and even a mini film studio in the garden that Maurice spent hours in. Robin had quit the Bee Gees soon after our wedding and, while Maurice and Barry were continuing the band together, Maurice, always uncertain of his talent and lacking in confidence, started to do more of his own projects and also writing more with Billy. All of my family were musical like me and, in the years to come, Edwina would also come down to London, go to drama school and start a career in music, TV and theatre.

At the start of our married life, however, Maurice and I were kids playing at being grown-ups, which meant there was a lot of partying. I'd get home from work to find him drinking with any-one from Robert Plant to Rod Stewart and Dudley Moore. On the rare evenings we went to sleep at any kind of normal time, the doorbell would often ring in the middle of the night and he'd go down to start the party all over again. Often with Keith Moon. I loved socialising and drinking as much as any twenty-something, but couldn't keep up with Maurice's pace, so often went to bed long before him. But we were young, having fun and I'd fallen in love with Maurice because of his irrepressible sense of fun, not in spite of it.

We also became close friends with Ringo and Maureen after they moved into a house in the same cul-de-sac that Woodley was on. They were living in Surrey when I told Ringo that a house near us which backed onto a golf course was up for sale. Like us, they enjoyed how secluded the houses were, but also being close to central London.

Over the next few years, the parties, nights out and socialising were constant. There were shopping trips to Bond Street and

Knightsbridge, first-class flights and holidays to ski in St Moritz or watch the Grand Prix in Monaco. When Prince Rainier and Princess Grace invited us to a post-race event, Maurice and I had turned up with Ringo and Maureen to find everyone wearing diamonds, black tie and satin. We somehow hadn't got the memo and were casually dressed. But Ringo and Maurice had walked in without a care in the world, so I'd had to style it out too, despite feeling crippled with embarrassment at making a mistake like that. My twenty-first birthday was marked with a diamond Cartier bracelet from Maurice and a party with Tom Jones, Little Richard and the Bee Gees. It was a heady and unreal existence.

But I also quickly realised I was going to have to be the grown-up in my marriage. Maurice was almost childlike in his lust for life and unwilling to let the boring stuff drag him down. Cheques for thousands would be left lying casually around, he spent hours in restaurants having long alcohol-fuelled lunches – crashing his car on the way home from one of them – and loved shopping. Our house was filled with cameras, music equipment and expensive cars. I'd go out to work with a Rolls-Royce on the drive of Woodley, and get home to find an Aston Martin or a Bentley. Maurice needed so much looking after; I even ended up picking out his clothes for him each day.

I didn't question it, though, because I was so used to being the responsible one that our relationship felt familiar. Plus, I was preoccupied with where to go next professionally because my contract with Mickie Most was coming to an end and, while he wanted to renew, I was searching to finally do the kind of music

I really believed in and wanted to consider other offers that were coming in.

I knew I had to take a leap and push myself in new directions if I was ever going to become the artist I wanted to be. So, with Marian's support, I decided to split with Mickie. We'd had ups and downs, but were friends too and it was hard to feel as though I was letting him down. But I also knew Mickie would never agree to make the kind of material I wanted to.

'I don't know the reason,' he said to a journalist when the press discovered I was leaving EMI. 'I get on very well with Lu. We've made a lot of money and she's had a very fair deal as far as royalties are concerned.

'Maybe she's making the right decision. We'll find out in two years' time.'

Success can be measured in many ways. Money is just one of them. And now I wanted to work with people who really believed in me as an artist with more depth. And so I signed to a new label – one that I believed gave me perhaps the biggest opportunity of my career to date.

'Most people don't realise that Lulu has an incredible amount of raw strength in her voice and style,' my new producer said. 'I can't help but be turned on to the enormous amount of energy and enthusiasm she projects when she sings.'

His name was Jerry Wexler and he'd produced some of the most iconic music created by female artists in the Sixties. Jerry was the man who had reconnected Aretha Franklin to her gospel and soul roots for her hit records, including 'I Never Loved a Man (the Way I Love You)', and also produced Dusty Springfield's album *Dusty in Memphis*. And he had built a label that was synonymous with the music I'd loved since childhood, the home of jazz, soul and R&B, and artists including Ray Charles and Otis Redding.

I was signing to Atlantic Records.

# 32

# Wake Me Up – I'm in Muscle Shoals

The non-descript brick building at 3614 Jackson Highway, Alabama, had once been a coffin showroom. Now, it was home to Muscle Shoals studio and some of the greatest musicians of all time, creators of a sound that reverberated down musical history. Barry Beckett on keyboards. Drummer Roger Hawkins. Bassist David Hood. And guitarist Jimmy Johnson. Four white men who recorded with iconic black artists including Etta James and Mavis Staples, Percy Sledge and Wilson Pickett, as well as a slew of the biggest white ones like the Rolling Stones and Bob Dylan. Nicknamed 'the Swampers', they were joined in the studio by a master guitarist called Duane Allman when I got to Muscle Shoals to record my new album with Atlantic.

But they weren't the only towering talents I was working with. As well as Jerry Wexler, who'd helped make Atlantic a powerful player with brothers Ahmet and Nesuhi Ertegun, I was also working with Arif Mardin, producer of artists including Diana Ross, Carly Simon and Willie Nelson during his long career, and Tom Dowd, an engineer and producer who'd collaborate with everyone from Eric Clapton to Ray Charles and George Michael.

This was certainly not another day in the office laying down what I felt was lightweight pop.

I flew to the US in late August 1969 to sign my new contract, pose for pictures with Jerry and spend a few days with him listening to tracks as the final selection was made for the album.

'We want to bring out the power and texture in your voice,' Jerry told me. 'That's what we need to communicate.'

None of the tracks we listened to felt completely stand-out to me and all I can say is that, when you hear it, you know it. But I also wanted to defer to Jerry's superior knowledge. He'd reinvented Aretha Franklin. What did I know? The only song I felt really strongly about was 'Oh Me Oh My (I'm a Fool for You Baby)' – a track written by a Glaswegian called Jim Doris – that I'd taken to Jerry because I truly loved it.

I walked into Muscle Shoals in mid-September feeling so nervous I was sure I would throw up before I ever got out a note, and quickly realised that moving to Atlantic was like going from a fast-food joint to a Michelin-starred restaurant. While Mickie had laid down tracks in the quickest time possible, Jerry, Arif and Tim poured over every note, chord progression and instrument. The recording of 'Oh Me Oh My' was particularly challenging too because Jerry kept stopping me mid-line to ask me to sing again.

'Can you try it like this?' he might say and repeat the line as I searched for the tiniest change in his intonation or phrasing.

It was hard to relax, pour myself into the music and really channel what I was feeling or how I wanted to interpret it.

Now, these men were great. They produced hit after hit. Their methods were clearly effective. But to twenty-year-old me, so desperate to do well, so in awe of everyone in the room and the footsteps I was following in, it felt a little overwhelming at times. But, even so, working at Muscle Shoals was one of the highlights of my career and I loved so much about *New Routes*. Jerry, Arif and Tom let me really use my voice and experiment on tracks like 'Feelin' Alright' and 'Mr Bojangles'. Together, we produced an album I'm still proud of today.

I knew the release of *New Routes* in early 1970 was a chance for me to show who I really was to the audience who'd bought into me so far – and find a new one too. The pictures we shot for the artwork summed up my new direction. Gone was Lulu in a cute dress. Instead, I was photographed sitting at the side of the highway in my casual green shirt, olive trousers and brown patent boots. The pop girl smile was gone, replaced with the almost hesitant gaze of a young woman as I looked into the camera.

'Oh Me Oh My' was released as the first single in late 1969 and didn't do well in the UK, but got to number twenty-two in the US a few months later. The album, however, failed to make an impact when it was released, which felt like a body blow. Either the public didn't want this new kind of music from me or the Atlantic team had slipped up on the promotion. *Melody Fair*, my follow-up album with them, went much the same way.

But then, and now, I know the work I did with Jerry, Arif, Tom and the Swampers speaks for itself. I might beat myself up about what I did wrong, about the songs they might have found for me and the paths missed, but I also know we did good. Plus, I'm a Scorpio and we're supposed to be at ease with all the deaths and rebirths of life. So I did what I'd always done: picked myself up, dusted myself off and kept going.

## 33

# Is It Really Necessary to Waste That Kind of Money Shopping, Mrs Gibb?

*I* stood and stared at the answering machine as I tried to make sense of Betty's message.

'Marie! Marie! It's yer mammy? Why won't you talk to me?'
Silence.

'Marie. It's me hen. What's wrong wi' you?'

Silence. Then the sound of my mother's tearful voice.

'Eddie. Eddie. I think she's on drugs. She keeps sayin' the same things over and over.'

The answering machine was one of Maurice's latest toys and Betty had no clue what it was. There were other things, however, that she found far easier to get used to. And shopping was top of the list.

Eddie rarely wanted to leave Glasgow – or the drink – these days. But Betty was always keen to fly down for a weekend and see me. Whatever I suggested we do, though – a restaurant or a play, a museum or a film – I only got one reply: 'Shall we go shopping?'

I could more than afford to treat Betty by now and she loved to visit Bond Street whose high-end stores were a world away from the markets where she'd spent a lifetime, and thousands of hours, hunting for bargains. But while she was always keen to see me buy myself something nice, Betty found it far harder to let me spend a lot of money on her.

'£100!' she'd shriek. 'For that! That's criminal. You're not buying me that. But you should treat yourself. You deserve it. You work so hard.'

I didn't need my mother's encouragement. I was still sensible and Marian kept me as on track as ever financially, but I could now afford to spend in a way that would have blown my mind just a few years previously – clothes, shoes, jewellery. My wardrobe grew and grew until the day I was summoned to a meeting with my very sensible, very staid, accountant.

His name was Aubrey Beckman and he was a partner at Casson, Beckman, Rutley & Co. He had a voice like cut glass, public school manners and usually treated me like a kindly grandfather. But at this particular meeting, he clearly wasn't feeling quite so indulgent.

'Mrs Gibb,' Mr Beckman said as he sat behind his huge mahogany desk. 'I've been looking at your accounts and wanted to ask about your purchase from a furrier in Beverley Hills.'

My mind flipped frantically back through that trip. I'd done a lot of shopping. Ah yes. I'd had a bespoke champagne-coloured mini mink coat made. It had taken three fittings to get it perfect.

'Oh yes!' I said brightly. 'It's gorgeous.'

Mr Beckman looked at me icily.

'My wife has had the same fur stole for forty years Mrs Gibb. Is it really necessary to waste that kind of money?'

I left chastened, repentant and vowing not to waste any more money. At least not on fur coats.

# 34

# Ol' Blue Eyes Gets Talking

Ambition is a curious thing in a marriage between two people in the same industry. It can often end up as a battle, or with one partner – often the woman – dimming her light. But in my early twenties, I didn't dare admit I was ambitious, even to myself. Back in Glasgow, that was called being full of yourself.

The Bee Gees had reformed with Robin, gone back into the studio to make hit music and start doing big international tours again. But even though my singing dreams had been thwarted again by the reception of my work at Atlantic, I would not be deterred. When you've been so far up, coming back down is terrifying.

And, by now, it wasn't just a question of what I loved to do because, aged twenty-one, I was still financially responsible for a lot of people. My family, of course, but also Marian who needed the income I generated more than ever after she divorced. As did all the people working for me: my driver, musicians, accountant, PR, assistant and musical directors. I had gradually become more of a business than a musical artist and, once that happens, you have to keep going to support the infrastructure of people around you. They all needed financial security and it was important to me too because it made me feel safe.

Marian and I concentrated on work we knew would keep me earning: TV and big cabaret residencies. Las Vegas was home to the biggest – and best-paid – venues and I started flying over to do a month or six weeks of nightly shows. I also started a run of many years which saw me doing one, if not two, series of my own BBC show each year that positioned me firmly in the variety bracket. Marian might have started relatively late in the music industry, but she was well connected with the big bosses of light entertainment and steered my career ever more in that direction. I sang, danced and welcomed guests ranging from Mama Cass and Wilson Pickett to Aretha Franklin. I felt incredibly lucky to be in the orbit of such huge stars.

Acting was another area Marian wanted to develop and I co-hosted a show with Dudley Moore because the entertainment bosses had spotted a knack for comedy. Plus, I did guest spots doing sketches on huge shows like *The Morecambe & Wise Show* and *Monty Python's Flying Circus*, and a film called *The Cherry Picker* that included a bedroom scene filmed on a damp boat in Spain – just me, my leading man and a tiny cabin crammed with camera crew.

All I remember of that time after Atlantic is spinning myself forwards, not looking back, and feeling more unsure than ever, because if the music wasn't working, then who exactly was I? But even if Atlantic hadn't played out as I'd hoped it would, I just had to carry on regardless. There were also still so many highs in my career – some so huge they left me breathless.

During a stint at the famous Flamingo Hotel in Las Vegas, for instance, I returned to my hotel room one night to find several phone messages from Tom Jones. He was having drinks at a bar across the road and wondered whether Maurice and I wanted to join.

We got to Caesar's Palace and headed into the bar, only to find our path blocked by a giant security man.

'Where are you heading lady?' the guy drawled as we looked up at him.

'I'm here to see Tom Jones,' I said and, right on cue, Tom stood up to wave us over.

With Frank Sinatra standing beside him.

I'd like to tell you I can remember every word we spoke to each other, but I can't. The night passed in a blur of champagne and my memory is hazy. But I do know Frank and I ended up talking about singing.

'Do you do vocal warm-ups before a show?' he asked me.

'No. Never!'

Frank leaned forwards with a serious look in those famous blue eyes.

'It's important to warm up properly,' he told me. 'I can teach you. You have to look after your voice.'

Ambition is one thing. Being pushy is another. But I had yet to learn to distinguish between the two, and I'd seen so many people desperate for fame and to be connected to the famous. So, when Frank Sinatra offered to help out a young singer, I couldn't follow up.

I wouldn't make the same mistake again today.

# 35

# Ma Mammy Meets a Mormon

After years of chaos, something began to shift between my parents. And it was all down to my mother.

Growing up Protestant, we'd been taught to say prayers and we went to church every Sunday when I was small. All that changed, however, when some Mormons knocked on the door of the new house I'd bought my parents – a bungalow in a suburb on the outskirts of Glasgow – and Betty invited them in.

'I'm not sure what it was they said, but something just struck a chord,' Mum later told me. 'So when I went to a meeting, I realised this was what I'd always been looking for.'

Betty's conversion changed her profoundly. Not overnight, of course, but, bit by bit, the grinding sense of injustice and unhappiness that had always filled the air around her began to lift. She found a loving and supportive community, stopped drinking alcohol and caffeine, and even ended up becoming a teacher in the church – loving the studying, planning and prepping it involved. Plus, after years of beans on toast, Mum even finally learned to cook. Mormonism provided her with a community as well as practical guidance on how to make changes in her life for the better.

More importantly, Betty's new-found serenity started to defuse some of the charge between my parents. Of course, they still fought, but Betty was no longer looking to take out her unhappiness on Eddie. Her rage had never been just about his addiction. There was a hole inside her that she needed to fill with self-love, and now she started to do that. So, while my father carried on drinking, Betty didn't react as strongly to it now she had something else to focus on – a religion that made her feel fulfilled and connected in a way she had never felt before.

I was happy for her.

'Will you come to a meeting with me?' she'd ask occasionally.

But I always said the same thing: 'Sorry Mum. But it's not for me.'

Betty accepted it and didn't pressure me. What I didn't realise then was that she was a seeker who had found the spiritual connection that suited her. It would take me a bit longer to find mine.

# 36

# Are You Sleeping with Her?

The two touchpoints Maurice and I always had were music and family. The Bees Gees are some of the greatest talents I've ever known and seeing them at work up close is one of my most treasured memories. For me, they were, and are, among the world's most incredible musical talents.

Music poured out of the Gibb brothers at a speed which took my breath away.

'What will the next Beach Boys single sound like?' one of them might say after they'd got out the guitars. 'Let's see if we can come up with something.'

But while they often used artists who inspired them as a starting point, whatever they wrote always had that famous Bee Gees sound and the music would tumble out of them.

'How do you do it?' I once asked Barry.

'I'm just a channel,' he replied.

One afternoon, Maurice and I had gone to a studio to meet Barry and Linda so the boys could work on some material and, as they waited for Robin to arrive, Maurice had started playing. Without a word, Barry put down his mug of tea, picked up his guitar and walked towards his brother. It was just the spark of an idea, nothing fully formed, and yet lyrics poured out of him as Maurice layered on a melody. And then, as if by magic, Robin appeared at the door, walked in and seamlessly slipped into the harmony. The song was 'Run to Me' and I swear it was written in two minutes flat. I'd call that a stroke of genius.

The Gibb brothers were far funnier at home than you'd imagine. They had a gift for remembering the funniest jokes and scenes from movies which they would always insist on reenacting late into the night, at Barry and Linda's house in London. We would holiday often in Ibiza where the Gibb parents lived, which quickly led to me buying a house there of my own in 1969. We were young, we felt invincible, the world was at our feet and life was good, for a time at least.

But on a more personal level, bit by bit, as one year of marriage stretched into two then three, my relationship with Maurice started unravelling. It was so subtle at first that I refused to acknowledge it – the way Maurice needed looking after, the constant feeling I had to be the responsible one. But, more and more, what I'd been charmed by began to worry me as I realised I'd married a man who was completely different to my father in many ways, but very like him in others.

Maurice was never angry or violent, of course. He was a gentle soul. But, as time went on, it became clear that we had two problems. One was the amount Maurice drank because I'd realised it wasn't just social, it was compulsive. The other was his often complex relationship with the truth.

Early on, while I was recording at Atlantic, for instance, Maurice had done a West End stage show during one of the Bee Gees' splits. He'd co-starred with Barbara Windsor, and something about their relationship had bothered me. I didn't feel threatened by it. I knew whatever it was wouldn't dent his feelings for me, which sometimes felt almost too intense. But something about the way Maurice sounded when I called him made me suspicious, and so I confronted him about it when I got home.

'Are you screwing around with her?' I asked, heart in my mouth.

Maurice looked at me as if I was mad.

'Don't be crazy Lu! You're being paranoid. I'd never do that.'

I found out years later that he did. And there were other friends too that I felt he got a little too close to. I didn't know anything for sure, though, and didn't want to believe it either, so I just pushed it all down. But even I couldn't ignore Maurice's constant drinking. I knew the signs, feared where they might lead us and gradually slipped into my mother's role as I nagged, harangued and undermined Maurice, trying in vain to get him to admit the truth.

'Do you have to?' I'd say as he got up in the morning, staggered downstairs and poured a beer.

'Are you drunk?' I'd hiss if I met him after work for dinner with friends and he appeared glassy-eyed.

'I suppose you're going to tell me you're having another drink?' I'd snap when we got home from a night out. 'What is wrong with you? You talk such rubbish when you're drunk.'

The more time passed, the worse it got. I hated myself. I was turning into my mother and beginning to resent the feeling that I was morphing into a nagging, watchful wife as my love for Maurice changed. We'd always been sociable, but it felt at times now that Maurice was making sure we were never alone as he created a buffer of people and parties to keep us from standing still and facing each other.

I felt increasingly on edge and scared about our future. I'd always wanted children, but how could I bring them into a relationship that reminded me so much of my parents'? My worst fear was repeating what I'd experienced as a child. Maurice, however, refused to acknowledge the truth in any way and hid himself in more and more extravagant tales of the projects he was working on and the people he was collaborating with. I don't think he meant to lie. But somehow he got so wrapped up in his fantasies he couldn't see where they started and ended. We argued more and more, I felt increasingly unhappy and, without realising it was happening, I started to seek comfort in a friendship I'd forged.

Having a reliable hairdresser is very important in my business because you invariably have to run in, get sorted out and quickly leave in between work commitments. But while I adored Leonard Lewis, who had been doing my hair at his Mayfair salon, I'd also become increasingly frustrated by his habit of taking very long lunches. When I asked Leonard to recommend someone else, he told me about one of his junior hairdressers who was a great talent and had been his assistant until very recently. His name was John Frieda.

John hardly spoke the first few times we met. He seemed very serious and focused. But, as time passed, we started chatting more about the things that interested us – Eastern philosophy and meditation in particular. It had all flown over my head just a few years before, but now, as I tried to make sense of who I was and where I was going, I'd become more interested in the answers it might offer. I was never going to go down the route my mother had taken, but something ignited as John dived into those topics with me and we talked about authors we liked such as Alan Watts, Carlos Castaneda and, of course, Paramahansa Yogananda and his *Autobiography of a Yogi*. John was the polar opposite to Maurice and, almost without realising, I developed a strong attraction to this young guy. And it was reciprocal.

I felt incredibly guilty, but I couldn't untangle myself. John stimulated and inspired me. It didn't hurt that he was easy on the eye too. And while I'd talked to my mother a little about Maurice's drinking, I also knew she had accepted my father's alcoholism as a burden she just had to bear. I wasn't sure I wanted to do the same. Marian knew how unhappy I was too and, on one long flight back from the States, I'd opened up to her about how confused I felt – and how strong my feelings were for John.

'That spotty, bad-tempered youth?' she'd exclaimed. 'You're the only one who makes him smile.'

Blunt as ever. Then she wrapped her arm around me as I sat blowing my nose into yet another tissue and her voice softened.

'But I also see the two of you when you're together,' Marian continued. 'You both light up. Marriages are long and complicated and I'll support you whatever you decide Lu.'

It was inevitable that I'd eventually blurt out exactly how I felt about my marriage to John. I've always had a problem with saying what comes into my head without thinking at critical moments and John had looked at me kindly.

'You're not the type to live a lie,' he said. 'You have to make a choice. Because if not, this is going to make you ill.'

All I felt, however, was confusion.

# 37

# It's Not Working

'Are you thinking of having children?'

I'd known my doctor for years and was seeing him for a routine check-up. Maurice and I had been married for almost four years and it was an innocent enough question to ask a young wife. But the moment the doctor said those words, I burst into tears. There was no way I could consider getting pregnant when things with Maurice felt so difficult. I already felt like the parent. I couldn't bring another child into our relationship.

'Have you thought about speaking to a professional about this?' the doctor asked. 'I know a highly qualified psychologist who deals with this kind of thing all the time.'

Back then, I hardly even knew what a psychologist was and had never dreamed of asking for help. But I was desperate, and so I took the name the doctor gave me, went to see the psychologist and poured it all out hoping she'd come up with a neat solution.

'I think you already know the answer to your questions,' the woman said.

I stared at her. Wasn't she supposed to be the one who'd tell me what to do?

'Only you can decide what is best,' the psychologist told me. 'But you've got a long life ahead of you and you're so young. You don't have children. You could both make a clean break and start again.'

The idea of hurting Maurice like that made me feel sick.

'Maybe we could have some time apart and work things out?' I said in a rush, desperate to find another solution.

When the psychologist offered to talk to Maurice and see how he was feeling, he refused to even consider it.

'We're fine Lu. You're just tired. You've been working so hard. Let's take a break? A holiday will make you feel better.'

Hearing Maurice dismiss me like that only made me more determined. It was yet another of his fantasies and I wasn't going to let him fob me off this time. Something had to change. But despite pleading with Maurice to see the psychologist, he kept refusing. I felt increasingly panicked. I had to get him to see sense. Our marriage couldn't go on as it was. We had to be honest and see clearly what was happening. I wanted to save our marriage, but also knew I couldn't live as my parents had done, ignoring the truth as it stared me in the face. Maurice and I were lucky. We had money, the ability to find help and use it, but, as days stretched into weeks, he came up with excuse after excuse.

'I'm too busy in the studio.'

'I've got meetings all day in town.'

'I'm in the middle of writing. I can't break off now.'

'What am I going to say Lu? We're fine. You're overreacting.'

He didn't get it.

Maurice started to come to bed hours after I'd fallen asleep and would be up and out by the time I got up. We were living increasingly separate lives, but the more he hid away from the truth, the more desperate I became to drag it out of him. Those were the darkest days, when I well and truly morphed into Betty, trying to jolt Maurice out of his fantasy that things were fine, hitting out at him in frustration as I tried to make him see sense. But all he did was either look at me sadly or tell me I was imagining the whole thing.

'You're acting crazy Lu,' he'd say as I ranted at him in the odd moments when we were home alone together in between work, sleep and parties.

My body ached and I had test after test, convinced I had a physical illness. I didn't, of course; I was just filled with frustration as I tried to find a way to save our marriage, but needed Maurice to help me find it. Eventually, he told me he'd made an appointment with the psychologist and I sat at home waiting for him, coiled with nerves and hoping he'd seen sense.

'She doesn't understand why you and I are even seeing her,' Maurice said on his return home, as he walked over to the whisky bottle. 'In fact, she thinks you're the one who needs help.'

My body went cold as he spoke and that was the moment I knew my marriage was over. I'd done all I could; I'd tried to convince Maurice to help save things, but he was never going to be able to see clearly. As the Bee Gees prepared to leave for a US tour at the start of 1973, Maurice and I agreed that he wouldn't come home to Woodley when he got back and neither of us would speak to the press when they inevitably picked up on the story.

But, days later, Maurice spoke to a reporter.

'I'm still in love with her,' he said. 'I've done everything to please her. I should have loved us to have a baby. But she was always working.'

Three months later, he spoke to a journalist again and told them I was married to my career in an article headlined 'Life Without Lulu'. I was used to seeing my private life splashed across newspapers and had participated in that to an extent, always trying to be as open as possible because I knew people were interested. But, this time, the newspaper coverage felt too much and I decided to speak out.

'I feel that my personal life has been brought out into the open more than anybody else's recently,' I said. 'I know this is the price for being famous, but people should accept that we have feelings the same as anybody else. It can be terribly upsetting sometimes.'

That was an understatement. The relationship between publicity and fame can be healthy at times, destructive at others, and it's a dance young stars will always have to navigate. I'd always been prepared to talk to journalists and couldn't complain every time a story was told. But there were also limits.

I was lucky, though, as well. All I had to contend with back then were newspapers and magazines. Today, there are even more casualties in a world that has sped up so much, it's become a twenty-four-hour blur of headlines and clickbait. No one wants to listen to a young star complain, but no wonder some break given the pressure they are under.

Aged just twenty-four, I was getting divorced and felt both embarrassed about such a public failure, as well as guilty that I had let Maurice down somehow. I felt it was all my fault.

'It's not working,' I said to Betty on one call.

'It's not all about happiness,' she replied.

# 38

# Ziggy Stardust Weaves a Spell

Bumping into Ziggy Stardust at the Hallam Tower Hotel in Sheffield was certainly unexpected. I was sitting in the lobby with my producer John Ammonds discussing my next TV show when David Bowie appeared: white face, flame-red mullet, platform boots and thin as a whip. David had taken the accepted boundaries of how men looked, morphed them into Ziggy and set the world of music on fire.

'Lulu!' he said as he saw me, and his face broke into a huge smile.

David and I had first met properly after bumping into each other at a recording studio in Los Angeles not long after *Hunky Dory* was released. Billy had introduced me to the album and we were both obsessed. David and I had chatted warmly to each other as Iggy Pop, who was with him in LA, looked at me like a dog watching a cat sniff its dinner.

Soon after, David's music had gone stratospheric when *The Rise and Fall of Ziggy Stardust and the Spiders from Mars* launched him onto a worldwide stage and he'd just followed it up with *Aladdin Sane*.

'Are you staying here tonight?' he asked as we chatted in the Hallam lobby.

'Yeah. I'm working. Leaving tomorrow.'

'Come and see the gig tonight. We're at City Hall.'

The great David Bowie did not disappoint – make-up, costumes, the interplay between him and his band, plus the music, of course. The show was mind-blowing – although I'm not sure quite what John Ammonds made of it all. Middle-aged, with large glasses, a thick military moustache and often seen chewing on a pipe, John was more used to the sedate performances he produced for the BBC, and Bowie was off the scale. After getting back to the hotel, I left John to tuck himself up with his Dick Francis novel and went back to my room where a note was waiting for me: 'Come to the bar. We're having a party.'

I found David in the bar surrounded by his crew and entourage, his Ziggy make-up now slightly smudged and mullet damp with sweat. I couldn't take my eyes off him. He really did look like he'd come from another planet. But whatever nerves I felt disappeared as we started chatting. David was funny and intelligent, swooping from talking about Buddhism and Kabuki make-up to studying mime with Lindsay Kemp and the music we were listening to. The two of us were soon nose to nose, drinks in hand, chatting non-stop as someone played a piano in a room saturated by a now familiar mix of performance high meets hedonism. As we talked about music, what he was doing, where I was going with it all, the more captivated and at ease I felt. David drew me in and, even surrounded by people, made me feel like the only person in the room.

He was irresistible. So far from my type that I'd never thought of him as attractive before. But just a few months after ending the confines of a marriage, I was ready to be plunged into the spell that was David Bowie: sinuous and almost fey one minute, assertive and masculine the next, morphing in and out of character. He felt exciting, unpredictable. One minute we were drinking and laughing, the next we were singing Anthony Newley songs at the piano and I felt so at ease by then I even dared to suggest he sounded a bit like him. David loved him and it fascinated me. The boundary-pushing rock star with the most eclectic of tastes.

'You've got a fuck-off voice,' David said as we sang. 'I'd like to write a song for you.'

I looked at him in shock. I was the face of middle-of-the-road Saturday night TV, *Eurovision* and the Freemans catalogue. Now the great – and very cool – David Bowie wanted to write for me? I felt almost euphoric as we talked late into the night, slightly overwhelmed too at being the focus of such magnetic attention from someone I revered.

Who wouldn't be seduced by all that?

Very late, David and I went back to his room and it felt like the natural conclusion of an intense evening – although I'd probably never have dared had I been sober. But I also felt so at ease with him and it was clear we were both very attracted to each other. I didn't feel like another groupie, more like a contemporary in the same topsy-turvy industry he was in.

People have been fascinated ever since by what happened between me and David, but I've always skirted around it. Put simply: David took charge of someone who, tipsy on both the moment and a copious amount of wine, was happy to be seduced. I'm sure, of course, that I was one of his many lovers at that time. He was one of the world's biggest rock stars after all, but whenever we were together, David wrapped me up in his world. When I left his room early the next morning, however, I thought I'd never see him again.

But after closing my bedroom door, the phone rang.

'Lu?' David said.

'Yes.'

'Let's make a hit record.'

Tired and still a little bit woozy from the wine, his words woke me up.

'The labels don't get you and they don't get your voice,' David said. 'I do. We'll make a great team.'

Caught between trying to play it cool and complete disbelief, I could hardly get to sleep with excitement. David must have had too much to drink and couldn't have meant what he'd said. Could he?

But a few days later, I was sitting at home when the phone rang. It was him again. David wanted to fix a date to meet and I went to see him at the Hyde Park Hotel where he played tracks to me as we decided what we'd do. He called me a few more times after that, we spent more time together and then he invited me to see him at the Hammersmith Odeon for the final night of his UK tour in July 1973. Obviously, I agreed to go.

Of course, the atmosphere in London was even more electric than it had been in Sheffield. The crowd was at fever pitch and the Odeon was packed with musicians including Ringo Starr and Mick Jagger. Excitement and expectation hung in the air as we wondered what the brightest star of the moment would come up with. And David didn't disappoint. Amid costume changes and huge theatrics, he remained the fascinating puppeteer putting the crowd under his spell. And then, as the collective high reached a crescendo, he made a completely unexpected announcement.

'Not only is this the last show of the tour, it's the last show we'll ever do.'

The crowd went wild, David tore into 'Rock 'N' Roll Suicide', bowed and walked off stage. People were crying, shocked and disbelieving that their icon seemed to be saying he was through with music. Later on, of course, we'd realise that David was 'only' retiring Ziggy Stardust and would go on to keep reinventing and innovating for years to come. But as a group of us arrived at the Café Royal for an end-of-tour party, the music press had already nicknamed the event 'The Last Supper'.

The place was packed. Paul and Linda, Cat Stevens, Ringo and Maureen, Mick and Bianca, Barbra Streisand, Ryan O'Neal, Marc Bolan and Sonny Bono. And there, amid it all, was David sitting on a velvet throne wearing a sky-blue suit.

'I hear you're going to do something together,' Mick said as we chatted. 'It's a good move.'

Did Mick mean I was playing with the big boys now? Or I'd finally make the kind of music he approved of? I never did find out.

# 39

# Maybe You Could Lose Some Weight?

Arriving at Château d'Hérouville, a recording studio on the outskirts of Paris, a couple of weeks later felt like being plunged into a scene from a French farce. Justin de Villeneuve and Twiggy were just leaving after shooting the iconic cover image for David's next album *Pin Ups*. She had a tan and David was milk-bottle white so they'd got round the problem by painting a pale Pierrot-type mask on Twiggy's face and a tanned equivalent on David's. Amid all that, I arrived in a pair of denim dungarees with Marian dressed in her signature look that was one part Alexis Carrington, another Maggie Thatcher.

I had two days off work and David and I were going to record 'The Man Who Sold the World' and 'Watch That Man'. But if I expected an aristocratic backdrop, then Château d'Hérouville didn't match up. The very basic bedrooms were like dormitories, but at least the food was good.

Perhaps too good.

'Maybe you could lose a bit of weight,' David said nonchalantly as we sat together on the first night.

Ouch.

The old spectre of insecurity about my plump face – and slim rather than super-skinny body – reared up inside me. I knew David found me attractive. He'd shown me that. But I quickly realised that the man I was with now in France was very different to the one I'd got to know in the UK. This was Bowie in business mode: focused, efficient and keen to get to work. There was still the Ziggy hair and fashion, of course, but, stripped of his make-up, David revealed a new side to his personality: the boss. This was his domain.

'Why aren't you smoking?' he asked one day as we were laying down my vocal.

'Because I'm singing. I don't smoke when I sing.'

'You should,' he said. 'In fact, smoke more.'

He handed me an unfiltered Gitanes cigarette that nearly blew off my head and told me to keep smoking as I sang again, keen to make my voice even huskier, rawer and richer. I did, of course, as I was told, keen to see where he would take me. We went into the studio late each day to work into the night with the *Pin Ups* band including guitarist Mick Ronson, who was going to produce the tracks with David. The sessions were focused and disciplined, and, as we sat together to listen back, discussing how to change the intonation on the next take, lift his backing vocal or tweak mine, I wasn't thinking about Bowie the man, but Bowie the artist and producer.

Later, I found out he'd noticed me when 'Shout' came out because he couldn't believe someone so young had had the nerve to take on an Isley Brothers classic. So while there has been a lot of interest in our 'affair', it was really all about the music. As so often happens when you're working with someone creatively, it was intense, the music united us and we forged a strong connection for a short time. After so long with execs who'd never really got me, it felt as if David did. He believed in me and saw something other people had missed. That's why meeting him mattered so much. We created and collaborated in a way I hadn't before.

It took six months for 'The Man Who Sold the World' to be released because of our workloads, but David finessed the track and we also did a newspaper photo shoot – me in a black evening dress, him in denim culottes and those platform red boots – which was headlined 'The Odd Couple'. The press, as expected, couldn't believe Bowie was partnering with me, while Betty was convinced I was collaborating with the Antichrist.

As the release date approached, I knew I'd have to think cleverly about my look. Music's most avant-garde artist was collaborating with Miss Saturday Night Entertainment. It was time to do things differently and Marian and I sat down to talk about what that might be.

'I think I should look a bit more androgynous,' I said.

Marian leaned forwards.

'Good idea,' she said. 'Monochrome. Tailored. We could use cabaret and Twenties Berlin as inspiration.'

We soon came up with a new kind of look that I loved: a black suit, wide-collar white shirt and black fedora with a white ribbon. It was a strong look and perfect for this new adventure. Within weeks, the track was at number three in the UK and a hit across Europe. Suddenly, a new version of Lulu had emerged.

Cooler, edgier. And, just as I'd hoped, people suddenly saw me through David's eyes. They were taking me seriously, looking at me differently, and it allowed me to reinvent myself.

In demand for TV and radio, I travelled a lot and David was busy too, so we didn't see each other much over the next few months. But there was talk of an album, so, after meeting in London for a few recording sessions, I flew out to see him in New York in April 1974 to work on two tracks called 'Dodo' and 'Can You Hear Me'.

But, once again, David Bowie had morphed into a new character and was different to how he'd been in France. There was a new edge to him, and I spent hours waiting each day for him to arrive because he'd become so nocturnal. I've since learned this was the time when he started to seriously use cocaine, so it makes sense. But, back then, I didn't understand the change. I just knew I felt uncomfortable and, used to being constantly busy, didn't like the sense of hanging around waiting for the maestro to appear. I loved 'Can You Hear Me' and enjoyed laying it down with David, but left unsure what would happen next.

Not long after, he gave an interview and said he'd like to take me to Memphis to do an album.

'She's got this terrific voice,' he told the journalist. 'And it's been misdirected all this time, all these years. She's got a real soul voice – she can get the feel of Aretha. She just has it naturally.'

But it wasn't meant to be. David was getting lost in drugs, his star was shooting even higher, he was touring *Diamond Dogs* and working on *Young Americans*, which was released the following year. He also split with his manager Tony Defries and, in between all that, the material we'd recorded never surfaced.

'Why can't you stay?' he kept asking when I told him I was leaving New York, almost disbelieving that I could pack up and go.

But I didn't know how to just hang out and see what might happen. I'd never learned how to stop long enough to do that. And I also feared I'd drown if I stayed around him. As seductive as the thought of making an album with the great David Bowie was, I didn't really know where I was with him and I had a lot of other stuff going on. I'd been asked to do a James Bond song, for instance – and follow in the footsteps of greats including Louis Armstrong, Shirley Bassey and Tom Jones. Only a handful of artists had had this honour and the track had been written by two men I greatly admired: John Barry, who'd defined the iconic Bond sound, and my old friend Don Black who had written the lyrics. They'd already laid down the track by the time I went into the studio to do my vocal and I wasn't sure if I felt more nervous about doing such a huge track or John Barry's insane reputation, panache and style.

From 'The Man Who Sold the World' to 'The Man with the Golden Gun'.

But it wasn't just work that propelled me out of David's world. There was also someone at home who was drawing me back. And so I decided to go to him.

V

# 40

# I've Met My Match

Two years after arriving back from New York, I married John Frieda. From the moment our relationship had started, it felt like the kind of soul connection I'd longed for. I'd quickly fallen headfirst into it.

Betty – and the rest of my family – had all loved Maurice because no one could resist him. Plus, he was a Bee Gee and constantly told everyone how much he adored me. But my mother was slightly suspicious of John, who was much more reserved – and wearing a Saint Laurent silk shirt while driving a Mercedes the first time she met him. How could a hairdresser who was just starting out afford all that? I'm not sure if Betty thought I'd bought them, but I hadn't.

'Where does he get his highfalutin ideas?' she'd ask me.

Betty had no understanding of the career John was building, the fashion crowd he was a part of and, of course, the empire he'd go on to create. John wasn't your average hairdresser. He applied his study of the American architect Buckminster Fuller and the geodesic dome to the art of cutting hair. I'd never met a hairdresser like him. In fact, John was different to anyone I'd ever met. And after creating Joanna

Lumley's iconic 'Purdey' cut for *The New Avengers*, he was on the up and up.

I knew John was not only talented but ambitious. We'd both left our childhood worlds far behind and shared an intense work ethic. A few weeks before we married, John had opened his first salon with his business partner and fellow hairdresser Clifford Stafford which was an instant success. Plus, he was increasingly in demand to work with photographers like David Bailey, Barry Lategan and Richard Avedon on shoots for *Vogue* and other upmarket magazines, and had an ever-expanding client list of celebrities and top models.

More importantly, John was honest, kind and thoughtful in a million different ways. I'd met my soulmate.

We married at Hampstead Register Office in October 1976, a few weeks before I turned twenty-eight. John in a black suit and me in a pale cream halter neck wool dress designed by my fellow Scot Bill Gibb that I wore with a matching coat and turban. If I'd looked like something out of *Doctor Zhivago* at my first wedding, I leaned into *Lawrence of Arabia* for the second. I had to lie on the floor of the car to get past the photographers waiting outside Woodley, but the wedding itself – thankfully – was very low-key and we went back home afterwards for a family lunch.

Then the party started. Robert Plant and Ringo were there, Tom Jones, Harry Nilsson, Rod Stewart, Dusty and Bill Wyman too. At some point, Elton John also dropped in with Kiki Dee because although I didn't know him well, his manager John Reid was Glaswegian so we'd come up together as kids in music.

Very quickly after that party, however, all thoughts of up-all-night drinking and dancing were forgotten when I went to see the doctor because I was worried about putting on weight.

'You're pregnant,' he told me.

This was definitely not in the immediate plan. But John and I had talked about having four children, so we were ready to start our family, however unexpectedly. And with that, I plunged into my latest role: one that would consume me more than any other had, just as it does most women. I was going to be a mother and I was never happier than when I was pregnant with Jordan.

# 41

# I Want It All

'Has he had his bottle?' I whispered down the phone in the backstage area of a theatre in Dublin.

It was 1978 and Jordan was about a year old. I'd given myself three months off after he was born before plunging straight back into work. Musically, I'd done a succession of albums and singles which had blurred into one, none of them making any real impact, and I was now making career choices driven by whether I could fit a job into my new life at home. The residencies were less Las Vegas, more Bournemouth these days, so that I could get home in a few hours.

The hamster wheel I'd been on for years felt even more turbocharged now I was a mother. I'd finish late performing somewhere far from London and sleep in the car on the way home. We had a nanny, and Betty needed no excuse to fly down to see her precious first grandchild, but I still felt incredibly torn between Jordan and work however well I knew he was being cared for – guilty too that I didn't seem to be doing any of it well enough.

Even after having my own child, I could not conquer the habit I'd learned when I was young: never coming to rest, always being on and ready to work. I think the fragility of life and living one pay packet to the next was deep-rooted in my working-class sense of the world. However financially comfortable I was, that feeling was locked into me and there were still so many people depending on me too.

But it wasn't just about money. I simply didn't know who I was without work. I was a workhorse. That's what I'd always been and no one ever sat me down to suggest there might be another way. And I had no role models. Tearing myself away from Jordan left me feeling constantly on edge and I often felt overwhelmed. Having expected to find being a mother easy after all the caring I had done for Billy, Edwina and Gordon, I was crippled by worry with a child of my own: wiping Jordan's nose fifty times a day, worrying about every red mark or cough, wondering what more I could do to soothe him night after night when he was chesty and crying because of croup. My childhood habit of being on constant watch for danger went into overdrive too. Plug sockets, slides, roads, dogs, stairs: the list of potential threats felt endless, so I was very far off being a relaxed, earthy type. And, in some ways, I replicated what Betty had done with me – the watching, waiting and overprotection.

Balancing all that with work was tough. And while John was as devoted as I was when he was at home, his business was grow-ing fast and he was working incredibly long hours. Still only in his late-twenties, it felt like he was being catapulted ever higher in his chosen profession as I started to flounder, and the more compromised my career felt, the tighter I gripped on to it, grasp-ing at straws trying to keep my head above water, going down a plughole as my career dipped. But the cruellest twist of success? It's never measured across an arc of time, but on your last hit – or miss. And it felt as though I was having more of those now. I was still in demand, but the recording business felt as if it was gradually slipping out of reach.

John and I tried to talk about it all, but there never seemed to be enough time. He did, however, see what was happening.

'You're not happy with yourself Lu,' he said one day.

'Easy for you to say,' I snapped. 'You don't come up for air. You're never home for dinner. I'm the one always rushing back.'

When John went to bed and straight to sleep like always, I stayed awake for hours turning it all over. I'd never slept well as a child and still struggled as an adult.

But arguments were also soon forgotten because John and I were completely devoted to each other and, despite all my guilt and frustration, being a family of three also made me happier than I'd ever been. Finally, I thought, I had found who I was: a wife and mother. But what I forgot is that there was a whole person inside me who still needed to be properly understood. For now, though, all my focus was on John and Jordan, hurling ourselves through the working weeks, spending Sundays at Woodley together or John's cricket fixtures, and holidaying in Ibiza.

When Eddie was made redundant from the meat market, it made sense for my parents to move to London. It was a huge wrench for them to leave Glasgow, of course, but, by then, Edwina, Billy and I were all in London so Betty and Eddie wanted to be close to us, and Gordon, who'd soon leave school, came with them. But while I offered to buy Dad a butcher's to run as his own business, he had no ambition to be his own boss and got a job in someone else's shop in north London instead. My parents moved to Chingford in Essex: Eddie still working and drinking, Betty more than happy to spend hours on buses trundling to Hampstead to look after Jordan because neither her nor Eddie could drive and they refused to have lessons. But at least the fire between them was far more subdued than it had been when I was a child, and I was happy to have them close.

My punishing work schedule continued and, in the summer of 1979, I started a season at the Winter Gardens in Margate when Jordan was two. After renting a house nearby, Mum came down to help and Edwina joined me as one of my backing singers. But three months in, I drove myself home exhausted one night on an unfamiliar road with fog rolling in from the sea, crashed headlong into another car and woke up lying in a pool of blood with a severe head injury. The other driver was also badly hurt; something I've regretted ever since. Bleeding heavily, I was rushed to hospital where surgeons put thirty stitches into the head wound before telling me later that I was lucky to have survived the crash.

So what did I do as I was wheeled out of the operating theatre, groggy and in pain? Signed an autograph for a cleaning lady. Within just a few weeks, I was back at work.

# 42

# The Truth Hurts

I'd known Pete Townshend for years. He was one of the
originals I'd come up with in music – bands and artists like
the Animals, the Kinks, the Hollies, Led Zeppelin, Eric and
Cat; men who were all my contemporaries and I'd watched
climb higher and higher. We'd long ago left behind the days of
being in and out of each other's worlds at the Blue Boar, parties
and gigs, but I remained fond of them all. John Lennon's
murder had felt not just brutal and inexplicable, but a very sad
severing of a time when it had seemed we could rule the world.

But now, as I looked at Pete a few years into the dizzying mix
of trying to combine family and work, I felt crushed, humiliated
and angry.

'What are you doing?' he'd said as we were having a drink
after appearing on a TV show together. 'Why are you doing all
this stuff? What happened?'

I stared at Pete.

'So what should I be doing?' I hissed.

'Music. You're a singer. And a good one.'

'You mean going out on the road like you all do, leaving my
family at home? I have responsibilities.'

Pete looked at me and shook his head.

'You've taken the easy way out. Sold out.'

Every molecule of five-foot-two-inch me bristled as I stared up at him.

'Don't lecture me. I've got a mortgage to pay. A family. It's not that simple.'

'It isn't?' Pete asked.

Deep down, I knew he was right, of course. And he wasn't the only one who felt that way. Billy did as well, and our relationship had suffered because of it. He felt passionately that I should be doing more music, trying to reconnect properly with that part of my career. But I just kept diluting it all and had gone down a plughole of TV and cabaret, taking me ever further from my roots in rock music.

'It's just more of the same Lu,' Billy would tell me. 'Why aren't you pushing yourself? Doing what you really love?'

I told my brother what I told Pete that night. That I had financial responsibilities, obligations, a family I had to take care of. But that wasn't the whole reason I'd got so lost. Marian and I just kept scrabbling forwards with as little strategy almost twenty years in as there had been when I was a kid. Marian was a product of a generation who didn't yet understand that collaborative writing would develop vocal artists and I still lacked the confidence to believe that anyone would hear what I said. I'd agreed to all the alleyways we'd gone down too – bits of this, bits of that, no real focus on music. I was as much to blame for what had happened.

It would be a long time, however, before I admitted all this to myself. Because while my resilience has been a blessing that's enabled me to keep going for sixty years when so many women like me disappeared long ago, it's also been a curse. Sometimes stopping – just for a while – is what you need to do.

And I refused to.

# 43

# What Are You Doing in My Wife's Wardrobe?

I hadn't quite morphed into Margo from *The Good Life* yet, but I was getting close. As John became more and more successful, I was turning into a Hampstead housewife, immersed in Home Counties cricket matches, the school run and swimming lessons.

'Why don't you dress like the other mummies?' Jordan asked me after school one day.

I'd looked down at my leather trousers and decided to change my look. I understood how it felt as a child to believe your parents were different to everyone else's and long to fit in and be the same. The leather went in the bin and soon I was drowning in shoulder pads and mumsy huge hair as the Eighties, its excesses and fashions, rolled on. My hair – and everyone else's – got so bouffant that I swear me, John and George Michael all had the same cut at one point.

By now, John had opened a second salon in Mayfair and his world was filled with the kind of women who dripped in designer labels and wore the uniform of the wealthy. I never felt lesser than – in fact, I often wondered just how all those ladies could bear so much lunching together – but I did what I'd done with Marian all those years before and moulded myself to fit this new world of wealthy wife and mother, desperate as ever to create structure and safety, to be who I thought I was expected to be.

It had felt like I was getting out of the career doldrums when I got offered a new TV show in 1981 called *Let's Rock*. It was produced by Jack Good, a visionary who'd originally brought rock and roll to British and American TV. I'd grown up watching his shows, and the new series was set in the Fifties and built around rock and roll, the production was high quality and Jack Good was also a fascinating man – a seemingly shy intellectual who dressed like a Teddy Boy – so I was so looking forward to working with him.

But my recording career continued to be uneven. After being signed to Elton John's Rocket Records, I'd made a soul and disco-infused album called *Don't Take Love for Granted* in the wake of *Saturday Night Fever* changing the musical landscape. My heart had filled as I'd looked on as Maurice, who had very happily remarried soon after we split, and his brothers dominated the scene. *Don't Take Love for Granted* was produced by my old friend Mark London, who was by now married to Marian, and Lem Lubin. It contained some great songs that I loved recording, but, once again, failed to chart.

But then, around the time of *Let's Rock*, I had signed to a new label who decided to release one of the *Don't Take Love for Granted* tracks as a single in the US. 'I Could Never Miss You (More Than I Do)' got to number two, I made a new album and 'Who's Foolin' Who?' earned me my first Grammy nomination for Best Female Rock Vocal Performance in 1982. I lost to Pat Benatar, but to suddenly be recognised for my music again felt like a very unexpected – but welcome – surprise.

Maybe all was not lost.

For a brief moment, it seemed as if America might beckon again. But any chance to capitalise on the upward curve disappeared when my new label ceased trading there. If some lives are measured in coffee spoons, mine is a series of deals, contracts and labels that have merged one into the other – often involving anything from agent disputes to personnel changes and buyouts which made music with potential disappear. I was much happier with the material I was doing now, but it just wasn't breaking through.

I continued to be in demand to perform abroad, however, because I was a recognisable face with a back catalogue people wanted to hear, so, although my recording career was up and down, I travelled a lot to perform. I toured the Middle East, Asia, Australia and New Zealand, and even found the time to start hosting my own show on Capital Radio. But in between it all, I also did some very questionable TV – including one show on which I sang a Neil Diamond track while riding a bloody horse. Within a few years, I'd also do an album called *Shape Up & Dance* that tapped into the aerobics craze. My face is going red even now. It was a low point.

This business really is a game of two halves.

Amid it all, though, a collaboration started which I still look back on with joy – and so much laughter. I'd known Kenny Everett since the early days when he was a radio DJ and permanently in the middle of whatever party was going on because he was obsessed by the Beatles, and Lennon in particular. Kenny was the same in private as he was in public: zany, irrepressible and hysterical. His mind darted constantly in different directions, he was incredibly creative and John and I had become close friends with him and his partner Nikolai, often enjoying long dinners together at San Lorenzo or Langan's. And by the early Eighties, Kenny had morphed from radio DJ to master physical comedian with a hit TV series.

'You should be on my show,' he suddenly exclaimed one day. 'It will be such fun darling!'

I'd never felt at ease in comedy because even though I'd worked on sketch shows with some of the greats, playing the straight woman to funny men had always felt uncomfortable. I was never quite sure what I was there to do and didn't think I had a comic bone in my body.

'But you do!' Kenny insisted when I told him. 'You've got natural timing. And that's the most important thing.'

I looked at him over the one, if not two, or three, bottles of champagne that littered our table at Tramp.

'If you make me laugh then you can make an audience laugh,' he said.

I wasn't sure it was that simple. You can't teach or force great comedy. And Kenny's gift came so naturally, he didn't see how precious it was. In the end, however, after more flattery, persuasion and alcohol, I agreed to do a sketch with him. Soon, I was on set wearing a hot-pink Lycra catsuit with Kenny beside me in matching emerald green. We were playing two office workers chatting incessantly during a workout class, Kenny throwing the stuffed prop legs he so often used to such great comic effect over the exercise bar as I tried not to laugh.

But there was one crucial difference in my work with Kenny compared to the comedy I'd done before: instead of being his straight-faced – and slightly passive – foil, Kenny and his co-writers Barry Cryer and Ray Cameron had generously written me a part that required me to actively participate in the sketch.

I loved every minute.

I happily agreed to work with Kenny again because I felt he got me and it was the start of a hugely enjoyable collaboration. Teaming up with him on his must-watch show didn't feel like work and I threw myself into every part he wrote for me. A waitress throwing food – literally – into Kenny's lap before pouring a glass of wine over his head; a lingerie-clad wife whose husband burst into their bedroom convinced she was hiding a lover somewhere. The sketch was filmed for a Christmas special on a set built in a huge army depot outside Bicester and Kenny and I couldn't wait to get started.

'Alright, where is he?' he demanded as he walked into the 'bedroom' to find me lying on the bed in a négligée.

After searching the room, Kenny strode over to fling open the wardrobe door and his suspicions were confirmed: a man was hiding in there.

'What are you doing in my wife's wardrobe?' Kenny demanded.

'Waiting for a bus,' the lover replied nonchalantly.

'Who does he think I am?' Kenny cried. 'A fool?'

And, with that, a double-decker bus crashed through the set.

Surreal and unforgettable, Kenny was truly one of a kind. And his premature death from an AIDS-related illness was just one of the many painful losses that awful time created. I still wonder what Kenny would have gone on to do. Probably keep all of us – myself included – laughing for decades to come. I still miss him today. So much talent lost, so many wonderful people gone.

# 44

# Opposites Attract

Where I was talkative, John was reserved to start with. I wanted my house filled with pattern and colour, John could have lived in a Japanese monastery. He loved cricket, I couldn't concentrate long enough to get the hang of the game. I bought – and bought – on impulse, he considered every purchase carefully.

The list could go on.

But as different as parts of us were, we were also very similar too and there were many things that connected us: curiosity, spirituality, music, our love for Jordan and shared ideals. We laughed a lot too and also shared an intense work ethic. I got frustrated with John for his long hours, only to take on a huge amount of projects myself. But however busy we were, we talked multiple times a day. I also thought John's tendency to keep his feelings locked up, which made him seem quiet and reserved, was the perfect antidote to my outgoing but anxious personality. Because while the world thought I was perpetually sunny, I believed John knew the real me. Or at least as much of me as I dared show him because so much remained hidden, even to myself.

There was one thing, however, we always disagreed on: John's need to plan and execute our lives with precision. And as we sat in the sun-filled garden of Marian's thatched cottage in Gloucestershire, John was once again keen to plan.

'Have you thought anymore about another baby?' he asked.

I started picking nervously at the daisies scattered across the bright green lawn. I could hear Jordan burbling away inside with Marian and Mark about the game of Poohsticks he wanted to play at the river later. He was five now and, although I'd always lived in cities, I had loved discovering the country through Jordan's eyes and, for all the opulence of her London home, Marian's weekend place was simple. I loved it all the more because of that.

On the outskirts of a village with no neighbours and views over green fields, we often nipped there for the weekend to take a break from work and also the feeling that wherever we went in London we were somehow on display. I'd now been in the business for almost twenty years and John was London's hottest – and best known – hairdresser. Wherever we went, people spotted us, and leaving the city was also one of the few ways I'd found of making sure John turned off from work. Almost.

'I'm just not sure it's the right time for another child,' I said as I looked at him.

John's face fell slightly. I knew he wanted to add to our family. Part of me did too. But I wished at times like these that he could be less analytical because I was driven by emotion and something was stopping me from committing to having a second child.

Not that I had explained how I felt, of course. Instead, I made excuses: I was busy; John would need to commit to being around more. But the reason I didn't talk to him more was because, deep down, I was scared – and I felt ashamed of that. Every other woman seemed to have a child and immediately feel ready for another. Once again, I just didn't fit in. And while I'd got pregnant accidentally the first time, making a deliberate decision to do it again terrified me. Just as my past had snaked its way into the beginning of my marriage to Maurice, it did so again now. I think, on some level, I was scared of tempting fate a second time. I'd been lucky with Jordan. We'd always shared a close bond. But some unarticulated fear that I was bound to end up repeating my parents' mistakes stopped me from daring to believe I could have another child.

John's face turned dark.

'Will there ever be a good time?' he said, his voice clipped and impatient. 'We always said we'd have another child and Jordan is five now. We can't wait much longer.'

'I know,' I replied. 'But the time has to be right.'

I got up and left him lying on the grass as I walked back into the house to find Jordan, unable to find a way to be honest with John about how I felt because I could hardly make sense of it myself.

# 45

# Rock Hudson, Zsa Zsa and Muhammad Ali

The word 'celebrity' today feels so paper thin, it has almost become meaningless. I've always believed there's a substance to being an artist or musician because you're grounded in a skill. But it's also true that some people who do those things end up 'famous', and there's a pecking order when that happens. While I've ricocheted between many of its layers, some people reach the pinnacle and stay there. Rock Hudson was one of them. A screen great, an acting legend, and now here I was sitting next to him beside his pool in the Hollywood Hills.

I had a new TV gig interviewing stars for a show called Some You Win hosted by Kenneth Williams. I'd chatted to Olivia Newton-John, who I knew from London; Muhammad Ali, one of the most consummate performers I'd ever met; and Larry Hagman with his Dallas co-star Charlene Tilton. I'd met Larry before at his Malibu beach house and, while the world associated him with his slithering Dallas character J. R. Ewing, I knew him to be an incredibly sweet man. He told me how mortified he was when he'd dried up on stage doing a sketch for the Queen Mother at the

*Royal Variety Performance and I understood how nerve-wracking it was. I'd done it aged nineteen and had kept thinking of everyone watching back home, which had made the whole thing terrifying.*

*'If you're gonna blow it, blow it big,' Larry had said with a rueful smile.*

*Zsa Zsa Gabor was a riot, like the kindest – and zaniest – aunt you could ever meet, a more extravagant version of Marian with even more glamorous diva energy pulsing out of her.*

*'You vant to choose something darlink?' Zsa Zsa had exclaimed in her distinctive voice after I complimented her on her outfit. 'Come have a look at my vardrobe darlink. It's very nice. No? You like pink? I love pink!'*

*Rock, however, was the one celebrity I was most excited to meet because I'd grown up with him. But I also felt nervous because the saying 'never meet your heroes' can be true. Some people can be deeply disappointing in real life – mean, charmless or just plain boring. Happily, Rock was as charming off screen as he was on it. And, also, perhaps the single most devastatingly handsome man I'd ever met, which was distracting.*

*'Shall we have a glass of wine?' he said as we chatted outside his beautiful ranch-style house once the interview was done.*

*This didn't feel like work.*

*I sat and listened to Rock talk about working with greats like Doris Day, James Dean and Elizabeth Taylor. But as glamorous as it all was, I mostly felt drawn to him because of something far simpler: his inner light. A pure, positive energy shone out from*

*Rock, who was funny one minute, reflective the next, charming and warm. I honestly felt like he could have been my best friend by the time I left late that day.*

*If only Hollywood and the Atlantic hadn't separated us.*

# 46

# Will I Sing Again?

'We'll work it out,' John said. 'We always do.'

'But it's eight shows a week,' I replied. 'It's a lot of work. What about Jordan?'

'I'm sure your mum will help and he can come in to see you on the days you're doing two performances.'

'You really think so? I want to do it but I worry about him.'

'Jordan will be fine,' John said. 'And you love a challenge. Always have.'

It was early 1983 and we were sitting in the kitchen at Woodley discussing a new project I'd been offered. Andrew Lloyd Webber needed a new leading actress for his latest show *Song & Dance* which was running at the Palace Theatre. I'd done a couple of productions of *Peter Pan* years before, but a one-woman soprano piece? By the man who'd done *Evita* and *Cats*? It was certainly going to be a learning curve.

*Song & Dance* had two acts. The first act, 'Song', was the one-act show *Tell Me On a Sunday* – the story of a girl who travels to the US and looks for love. Now, Andrew had combined it with a second act called 'Dance' – a ballet choreographed to a piece of his classical music with Wayne Sleep starring. I was longing to stretch myself, and the combination of Andrew's music, Don Black's lyrics and direction by John Caird, who had a background at the Royal Shakespeare Company, was very tempting.

'And you think I can do it?' I asked John.

He looked at me.

'Don't you always?'

I threw myself in and worked harder than ever to learn the part because while I'd always sung and danced on stage, this felt very different: no band or back-up singers to interact with – just me, an orchestra down in the pit and the audience out front. There was also the challenge of mastering the soprano material, and I trained hard with vocal coach Ian McKay to use the upper part of my range more than I ever had before. By the time opening night came, I felt nervous but prepared as I walked onto the stage. The evening went by in a blur – twenty-one songs and a final number dancing with Wayne Sleep – but I felt euphoric when the curtain went down and I could hear the audience still applauding.

The show also prompted a reunion that had been a long time coming. I hadn't seen Maurice since we'd split, but he came to see me with Barry and Robin. We'd finally come full circle and the love that remained was fond. There were new people too, like Freddie Mercury who came to see his good friend Wayne Sleep. We'd never really been in each other's orbit because Freddie came from the generation that had made it big in the Seventies. But he was a very cultured man who loved opera and ballet and ended up seeing *Song & Dance* three times.

When we were young – me, Edwina and Billy (1961).

Performing 'Shout' on television with the Luvvers.
(From left to right: Tommy Tierney, Jimmy Dewar, Dave Mullin, me,
Alex Bell and Ross Neilson, 1964.)

From posters on my bedroom wall to meeting John Lennon and Paul McCartney. (Recording *The Music of Lennon & McCartney*, 1965.)

Kicking our legs up for a press photo on the set of *To Sir With Love* with Sidney Poitier, Judy Geeson and Adrienne Posta (1966).

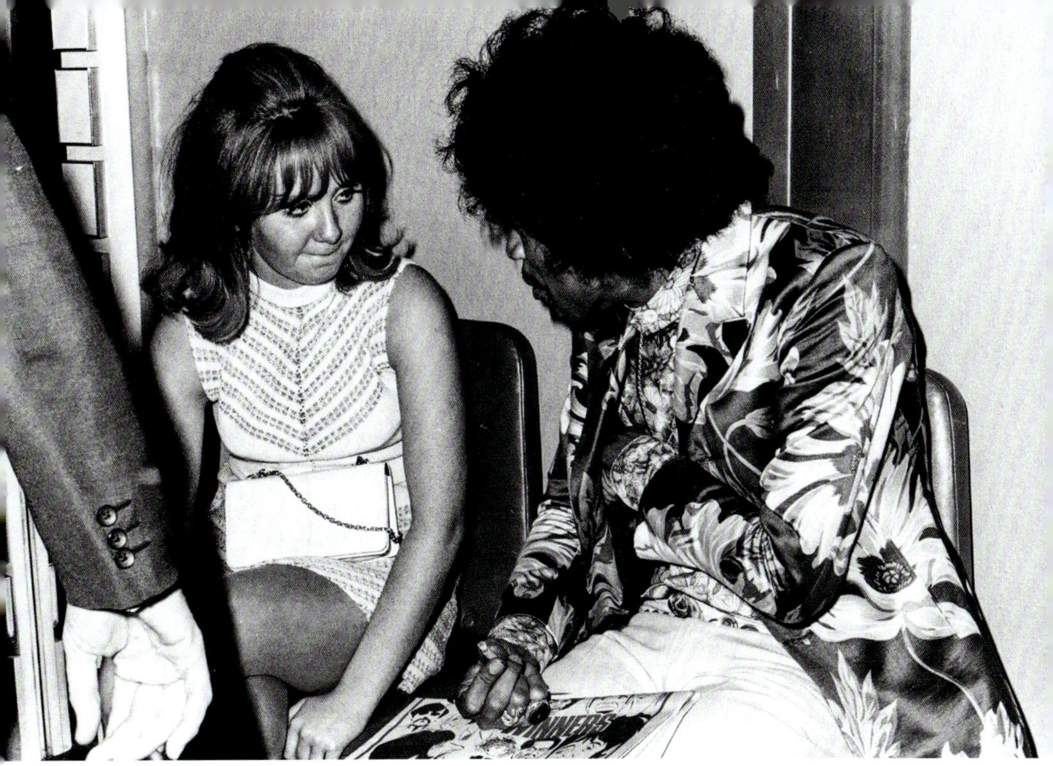

With Jimi Hendrix backstage after the Melody Makers Pop Poll Awards party (1967).

We won! Representing the UK at *Eurovision* in Madrid, singing 'Boom Bang-a-Bang' (1969).

Another night out in London with Maurice, Ringo and Maureen Starkey (1970).

What a night to remember. Celebrating in style after David Bowie's last show with Ziggy Stardust at the Café Royal (including Angie Bowie, David Bowie, Bianca Jagger and Edgar Broughton in the back row, and Maureen Starkey, Mick Ronson, me, Jeff Beck, Celia Hammond and Ringo Starr in the front row, 1973).

*An Audience with Lulu* with my mentor, Elton John, and Maurice Gibb (2002).

Jordan pinning my OBE onto my coat in the grounds of Buckingham Palace (2000).

With my sister, Edwina, doing a sponsored walk to raise funds for
my mental health trust (2025).

Filming a scene in the world of Ab Fab for *Absolutely Fabulous: The Movie*. (From left: me, Gwendoline Christie, Jennifer Saunders, Abbey Clancy, Joanna Lumley, Sadie Frost and Tinie Tempah, 2016).

Appearing in the Take That Odyssey Tour (2019).

Paul McCartney and me in the control room at Abbey Road Studios in 2024 while doing backing vocals on a couple of Paul's recordings.

One of many festival performances in 2025.

Having a ball on the Pyramid stage with Rod Stewart while performing with him at Glastonbury, 2025.

'I love you in this role darling,' he said to me backstage. 'And your voice sounds amazing.'

You get a lot of smoke blown up your arse in my business and it can often feel hollow – no one can do anything but great work. I'd certainly had my misfires, but getting affirmation from certain colleagues was always meaningful to me, and Freddie was one of the greatest performers of his generation. To have him enjoy my performance in a new medium meant a lot.

But about a month into the run, I was singing on the top of the set above the orchestra when a foldback monitor failed and I couldn't hear myself. Singing louder and louder, I forced my voice and, within days, my high notes were no longer clear and sharp. When my voice went hoarse, I had to cancel my appearance and felt as if I was letting everyone down, especially myself. In two decades of performing, I'd only ever cancelled twice before. I was never an unreliable, mercurial star. My work ethic made that impossible. I always turned up where and when I was expected to and put on the best show I could.

Consultants advised me to rest my voice and not to speak for a couple of weeks. Given that I hadn't shut up in the whole thirty-five years of my life to date, it was hard. Almost worse was the fact that I could only communicate by writing notes, which tested my very limited patience to the absolute limit. But I told myself it was just temporary. I'd always sung, and I'd never had problems. As one week stretched into two then three and four, however, my voice didn't recover and an ENT specialist told me I had nodules on my vocal cords and advised me to have an operation to remove them. He even showed me the long – and very thin – scissors he'd use during the procedure.

John was appalled. He couldn't understand why I wasn't flying off around the world to get second opinions, instead of trusting someone I'd only just met. But there was something about the doctor, Mr McKay, that made me feel fully confident in his opinion, so I had the operation and went home to recuperate.

But during those long, often lonely, weeks resting at home after the operation, I finally started to panic. What would it mean if I couldn't sing again? Who would I be? That should have been enough to ring alarm bells. Music was important, so was my work, but the fact that I couldn't imagine who I'd be without it was a sign I refused to acknowledge.

Marian was as concerned as I was; worried about me, of course, but also about her income because I was her only client and the way our deal was structured meant she actually made more money than I did. It didn't bother me. I'd never been in it just for the money and I felt like I had plenty. I also saw Marian as my business partner. I wouldn't have a career without her, I told myself. John told me I was mad and looking back now I realise that, like a lot of artists, I didn't take enough interest in the money side of my career. But back then it somehow all made sense to me.

Now, as I waited silently to see if the operation had worked, I ricocheted between intense worry and overwhelming annoyance at still having to write those bloody notes.

'Of course your voice will recover,' Marian would say when she came to see me. 'The specialist just said we need to be patient. It will take time.'

And then Marian would sit, just as she had done for so many years, and soothe me with a constant stream of industry chat, the odd bit of gossip and her excitement about all the new projects I'd soon be doing.

I rested, waited and forced myself to stop panicking about what ifs. Six long weeks later, I sang my first fragile notes, but they sounded so weak and reedy, I was filled with fear again.

'I've read about a brilliant woman,' Marian soon told me. 'She's called Helena Shenel – she's worked with Annie Lennox and George Michael and is the best in the business.'

She was. Helena worked with me over the next few months and I still thank her every day for the lessons she taught me.

'You know how to sing,' she said the first time I met her. 'But what I will teach you is the technique to access the full range of your voice and never harm it again. You'll learn how to drop your jaw, breathe and support any note because each one is as important as the other.

'And together we will reveal the extent of your true range with no fear of damage in the future if you follow my instructions.'

Helena was right. Even today, my voice is strong and hasn't deteriorated in the way some have because she finally managed to teach me what Frank Sinatra had offered all those years before: to protect my vocal cords.

The following year, I was offered the role of a lifetime: Miss Adelaide in Richard Eyre's celebrated revival of *Guys & Dolls* that had started out at the National Theatre and was now transferring to the West End. After a tour of regional theatres, we returned to the Prince of Wales to do seven months of shows which started in June 1985. It was a truly magical experience. Adelaide was the dream role, the choreography by David Toguri was masterful and the music pure joy from start to finish.

I still look back on that time as one of the happiest of my life. Jordan would come and do his homework in my dressing room while I got ready for the show. And then I'd go on stage and be lifted up by working in such a landmark production with a talented cast. It was hard work and nerve-wracking, but I held my own. I had morphed once again and could now add 'leading lady' to my CV.

# 47

# There's More to Life

I sneaked a look at my watch. Fifteen minutes felt like a lifetime. John and I were sitting in a large meeting room in a building on Harley Street – women grouped on one side and men on the other. But while my husband looked as if he was actually making this meditation thing happen, I kept glancing at my watch, panicked that I'd never be able to get to grips with it.

John and I had always been looking for a teacher to show us how to meditate. But things changed when he did a big hair show in New York and needed help with the models because they were going to be wearing huge dresses – and hair – and had to walk exactly right. I was still doing *Guys & Dolls* and David Toguri had put us in touch with a young woman called Candy Darling, who was dancing in *Dreamgirls* on Broadway. If you've worked with dancers then you know they are the hardest workers in any show, but something about Candy intrigued John because amid all the frenetic, highly strung preparations, she'd remained completely calm.

'How do you keep your cool in the middle of all the drama?' he'd asked her when they all went out for dinner.

'Siddha Yoga meditation,' Candy replied. 'There's a centre in London if you want to try it.'

John being John, and also someone who ran permanently on nervous energy, immediately threw himself into learning everything he could after getting home. Busy at the theatre, I couldn't go with him much, but did read a copy of *Where Are You Going?* by Baba Muktananda and one idea had deeply resonated: instead of looking outside for the answers, we have them on the inside. In the mid-Eighties, the decade of material-ism, yuppies and excess, that idea stopped me in my tracks and I cried joyful tears that came from somewhere deep inside me. A recognition of the truth.

In all the years of being whoever it was I was told to be, of fitting into the shapes other people had given me and distracting myself from the past, I hadn't thought a lot about my internal life, too often caught up in focusing on the outside, smiling and performing. And not just at work. In everyday life too, people often wanted some-thing of me: an autograph, a chat, a picture – or even just had a long, hard look. And it only fed the feeling that I constantly had to perform the part of 'Lulu': smiling, convivial, happy.

It was exhausting to always be on.

The idea that I had all the answers on the inside and just need-ed the tools to slow myself down long enough to access them both fascinated and resonated with me, as did the knowledge that I could connect to that part of myself I had never truly discovered before. My inner self. But the problem is that none of this is an easy fix. Learning to meditate takes devotion, determination, focus and vigilance. My mind had raced since I was a child and now I had to somehow still it? Impossible. It was doing cartwheels once again now as I sat in the Siddha Yoga Meditation Centre, but two things made me determined to keep going,

The first was that I felt unusually comfortable. There was a wide mix of people at the centre – doctors, students, nuns, a rabbi, all ages and stages – but none of them were that interested in me. Instead, we were all united in one purpose: to learn. So, despite my difficulties, something inside told me to stick with meditation when we left that day. Call it instinct. I just knew I had to pursue this and be disciplined. I started to learn all I could about meditation and its allied disciplines – all forms of yoga, chanting and pranayama breathing exercises – as well as studying ancient texts including *The Bhagavad Gita*, *The Upanishads*, *The Yoga Vasistha*, *The Vedas* and *The Mahabharata*. I only felt brief moments of the kind of stillness and connectedness that teachers talk about. But it was a start and I knew I wanted to experience more because the only place I'd ever felt that way before was on stage. The idea that I could feel peaceful in everyday life truly felt like a light bulb turning on inside me.

The second thing was seeing the head of the Siddha Yoga Foundation Gurumayi Chidvilasananda for the first time when she passed through London on her way from India to America. John and I went to see her. Incense was burning and people were chanting as we sat in the lotus position and waited. I'm not sure what I expected, but certainly not the most beautiful woman I'd ever seen. This wasn't skin-deep beauty, however. Gurumayi radiated an other-worldly energy that took my breath away as she settled into her chair. I could feel the most profound stillness and serenity sweep over me in her presence. The meaning of the word 'yoga', I'd come to learn, is 'to unite'. Siddha Yoga and meditation had nothing to do with what people do in a gym. It was about developing the practices that help you strengthen the unity of mind, body and soul. And Gurumayi captivated me because she embodied them.

When I went home and sat for meditation, as I had done so often before, I was plunged into complete stillness for the first time, my mind and breathing finally slowing down. After all the years of being on alert, the watchfulness and rushing thoughts, I felt a very powerful shift in me and knew this experience would be important to the rest of my life. What I later learned is that I had experienced 'shaktipat' that day: the moment when a spiritual master awakens another person's innate spiritual power, or kundalini.

I didn't have all the answers yet, of course. I still haven't. But I have some. And forty years on, I'm still learning every day. But, back then, I finally started to dismantle so many of the ideas I'd been taught – and top of the list was the idea that financial wealth, external success and marriage to the right man would solve all my problems. I started to see that I needed to become whole in myself and could go inside to find my own solutions by meditating. After years of being trapped in many ways by the past, I began to glimpse a way through. A new beginning.

And my spiritual journey, the sense I had a whole inner world to nourish for perhaps the first time, could not have come at a better moment. Because although life felt stable back then, its twists and turns were far from over.

VI

# 48

# Time for Change

I was on a high after finishing *Guys & Dolls* when Marian told me a record label had approached her with an idea. They wanted me to release a new version of 'Shout'. It was a classic pop song by now and a new generation were still listening. Jive Records had been co-founded by Clive Calder and Ralph Simon, two titans of music whose label would go on to champion huge hip-hop artists in the Eighties like A Tribe Called Quest and dominate the charts with pop acts including Britney Spears in the Nineties. But, however accomplished they were, I wasn't sure about the idea.

'It's years old,' I said to Marian. 'I was doing it as a Sixties kid. Surely we can find something newer, fresher?'

Marian was convinced of the plan though. Doing an updated version of 'Shout' would guarantee me a hit. And it had been a while since I'd had one of those. So, despite my misgivings, I gave in. Had anything really changed since all those years before when I was convinced to do material I didn't believe in?

No.

I was still the same odd mix of assertive and decisive when it came to actually performing, yet hesitant and biddable in the face of people who I thought 'knew better' about strategy. I trusted Marian completely and the Jive execs were very experienced.

I'd been saying yes for so long that I still didn't know how to say no. And, like I said, starting on a spiritual path doesn't mean you work everything out overnight.

They say that parts of people who become famous at a young age can get stuck there, and I certainly agree that being in the public eye as a child or young teen is always going to have an impact. It certainly had on me because it's an unreal existence – adored in one way, pulled down in others. There are drugs, alcohol and people who want to be in your orbit simply because of what you represent, not who you really are. If adults have a hard time keeping up with it all then what chance do young, unformed performers have?

But I also believe that early fame affects some young people more than others, and my past meant that I remained in many ways a fifteen-year-old jumping to everyone else's tune. When the new version of 'Shout' was released in July 1986, I felt pulled back into that old familiar robotic performance mode when I appeared on *Top of the Pops* to sing it. As it started climbing the charts, though, I didn't have time to dwell because John was suddenly rushed to hospital.

Married for ten years by now, John's career had only continued to expand and he had three salons, was ever more in demand and also planning his own haircare line. Funding a new business, however, was going to be expensive so we'd agreed to sell Woodley. The busy London traffic also meant John spent hours in the car commuting, and moving into Mayfair around the corner from his salons made sense, so we bought a large apartment there. But when the buyer for Woodley pulled out, we were left with two homes – and mortgages. John, always a compulsive worker, went into overdrive as he put in more hours than ever to fund a bridging loan.

He'd always had stomach problems, but would never see a doctor however much I asked him to. For months, I'd been worried that he was pushing himself too far and, in mid-July, he was suddenly rushed to hospital with a perforated ulcer. After undergoing emergency surgery, John contracted an infection and, for ten long days, I was terrified he might not recover. It was weeks before he finally left hospital.

Between home and work, life felt like a blur. Marian and the execs were proved right when 'Shout' got to number eight, but I got no joy from being back in the charts. I loved 'Shout', I always will, but rereleasing it after the high – and forward momentum – of my stage work felt like a backwards step. When plans were made to record 'My Boy Lollipop', I was on the back foot yet again because the rerelease of 'Shout' had been a hit, just like they'd said. I agreed to the plan, but the humiliation I felt deep down is indescribable. It's one thing to do material that infantilises you as a young adult, it's another to still be doing it after nearly twenty-five years in the business, married to your second husband and the mother of a nine-year-old. I think I wasn't in my right mind.

I'd made some fantastic music. I'd also done my fair share of shit. But this felt like rock bottom. Marian was still urging me to take the execs' advice and maintain a public image I helped feed as the bubbly, ever-youthful 'girl' of pop. I felt so frustrated, and while Marian and I had always got through any difficult moments in the past, tension started to build between us now as I got more and more unhappy about our inability to find a way to innovate. We were repeating the same – old – mistakes. And if that's not the definition of madness, then I don't know what is.

My fatal flaw though? Handing over my power. Not realising that some part of me was actively choosing to let myself be pushed into an ever-tighter corner. Because then I'd finally be forced to look at myself. And I'd have to change.

# 49

# Bob and Paula's Wedding

B ob Geldof and Paula Yates' wedding was like a who's who of music. All of the faces were familiar, but many came from a new generation of stars. The Sixties, Seventies, and now the Eighties ... each decade redefined by a new surge of British talent. Everyone from Duran Duran to Spandau Ballet had packed into the church near the Geldofs' home in Kent. George Michael, Midge Ure and Sting were there too – a new wave of artists taking over the Eighties with their distinctive sounds.

With John now out of hospital, we'd been invited to the wedding because he did Bob and Paula's hair. I'd always loved Bob's irreverent sense of humour and kindness. Paula, as ever, was dressed to impress in a dramatic scarlet frock. Eric Clapton and David Bowie were also among the guests, but I can't even remember seeing them. Someone told me later that David thought I was angry about what had happened between us, but I never was. We'd meet again years later, smile at each other and put that ghost firmly to rest.

After Brian Aris had taken his iconic shot of Bob and Paula surrounded by a gaggle of stars, the celebrations had started with a game of baseball before the party kicked into another gear after we'd eaten and the dancing started. The atmosphere was joyful, electric, and soon an impromptu jam session kicked off as it spun ever higher into the ether. Bob got on stage with Simon Le Bon and George to do 'Twist and Shout', Kevin Godley was playing the bongos, Midge Ure was on the guitar and I ended up on stage too with Chrissie Hynde.

Part of me felt catapulted back to those days in the London clubs when I was a teenager, surrounded by musicians on the up and up, united in that feeling of invincibility and euphoria. But as I sang, I also became aware that I couldn't join in with it. In fact, I felt uncomfortable, a step apart once again. I was back in the charts with 'Shout', I'd been doing it for more than twenty years and, in a few weeks, I'd release 'My Boy *bloody* Lollipop'. What must these guys be thinking? How stagnant could I get musically?

I might have been only thirty-eight that day, but after working non-stop since the age of fifteen, there were moments now when I felt a thousand years old.

# 50

# An Opportunity to Step into Julie Walters' Shoes

Stepping into a role Julie Walters had made her own was daunting because it still felt odd that 'actress' had been added to my now very 'portfolio' CV. Singing came naturally, TV presenting had felt like playing to my persona, comedy with Kenny did not feel like a day at the office and theatre was a natural evolution of what I had always done. But acting was a skill I didn't feel I had any right to try to claim.

I took a deep breath, accepted the part and threw myself in.

I was playing a down-at-heel mother in the second instalment of the *Adrian Mole* series – *The Growing Pains of Adrian Mole*. For someone who'd always put a lot of effort into looking just right, dowdy Pauline Mole was a shock – complete with dark hair and frown lines carefully drawn onto my face by the make-up team. The plotline revolved around Adrian's continued obsession with his girlfriend Pandora and chaotic homelife. His mother, Pauline, had left her husband in the first series to take up with a new lover and was now having a baby, which meant I had to wear a pregnancy suit as filming got underway. Still feeling ambivalent about having another child myself, I didn't think too much about it. But the arrival of the tiny babies who were going to 'act' the part of Pauline's new daughter changed things completely.

Three of them came on set with their parents to film and it felt like I was holding newborns for hours at a time. Cradling their tiny frames made memories come flooding back. I began to remember all the best parts of being a new mother and that all-consuming love you feel when you first see your child.

As filming continued, I was finally filled with a powerful feeling that I wanted to have another child. Jordan was ten now. I had spent so many years making excuses and being too afraid to admit, even to myself, that I wanted another child. If I didn't hurry up, he'd be leaving home soon and wouldn't have time to get to know a sibling. I'd grown very close to Edwina now she was in London, but knew I'd missed out on a lot with her and Gordon after leaving Glasgow when they were still so small. I didn't want that for Jordan. By the time the shoot had ended, I'd made up my mind. Those tiny TV babies had broken my defences. I was finally ready to have another child.

This time, however, I didn't get pregnant nearly so easily and it took two years. But in the summer of 1988, I found out that I was expecting my second child and was so delighted – I couldn't believe I'd spent all that time putting it off. John seemed over the moon too and I felt hopeful and excited for this next stage of our family because while he'd once said he'd retire by the age of forty, I was beginning to see that his ambition was far bigger than I'd ever realised. In fact, his drive to succeed was beginning to feel like a mistress taking all his attention, leaving little spare for me. I hoped another baby would push him to focus a bit more on family life.

But ten weeks into the pregnancy, I felt my stomach start to cramp as I stood on stage in Bournemouth for a new summer season I was doing. And after starting to bleed, I went to hospital where doctors told me I'd miscarried. I felt numb as I heard those words, disbelieving. My body had never let me down before and I irrationally felt it had somehow failed me. Losing a baby is to lose hope and a future you start to picture the moment you know you're pregnant. I felt heartbroken and, even worse, the press had already picked up on my pregnancy because I'd excitedly told the cast of the new show, so the papers were now filled with the story of my miscarriage. I was angry with myself for ever letting the information become public and retreated home. But while I'd intended to rest, my thoughts quickly felt too uncomfortable. I was turning forty in a few months and women didn't have babies at that age. Or so I thought then. Jordan might never have a sibling now.

And so I returned to the place that had always been a refuge, but also an escape. A week later, I was back on stage.

# 51

# Shellshocked

Betty stood looking around the flat John and I had just rented after selling our Mayfair home.

'It's a bit small isn't it?' she said. 'And dark too?'

The ground-floor flat was in the corner of a large building in Maida Vale, so light was certainly limited.

'It won't be for long,' I replied. 'We'll move somewhere bigger in a few months. We just needed to free up some money.'

Betty looked at me. I knew my parents would see selling our Mayfair apartment to help finance John's haircare business as a backward step. It was 1989 and he'd partnered with Gail Federici, a brilliant business brain who'd worked at the top of a big haircare company, to relaunch the John Frieda haircare brand in both the UK and the US.

The two of them were a perfect fit. Gail was as detailed, analytical and passionate about the gaps in the haircare market as John and together they were going to take on the huge companies by disrupting a weak spot in the market. They knew the products made by the big players to help women get big hair also contained ingredients that exacerbated another problem: frizz. So, they created a first-of-its-kind serum to solve it and were convinced Frizz Ease would be a big seller. They weren't wrong on that one.

Betty walked up to the window to look at the garden outside. Our new flat was in a mansion block set in a four-acre garden – huge for London – and it had all we needed: two bedrooms, a kitchen and sitting room. We weren't exactly out on the street.

'Jordan will be able to make friends and play out there,' I said. 'And this is fine for us for a while. John has always supported me Mum. I want to do the same for him.'

Betty looked at me sceptically. Her expression said it all.

What you learn, however, when clouds gather in your marriage is that it's never one person's fault. Together with a woman called Ann Bell, Gail and John were working all hours as they strategised and planned. Even when John was finally at home, he spent hours on the phone to Gail, who'd relocated to London from Connecticut with her husband Jimmy and twin girls. But while John's constant work was certainly an issue, my insecurity was another. Where once his focus had centred on me, I felt secretly jealous that Gail – and their business idea – was taking up more and more of his time. I didn't understand why Jimmy wasn't as annoyed as I was.

'I married a woman with drive,' he said one day as I complained. 'And while there isn't much space for us right now, we have to let them get on with it. This is who they are. And they're good people.'

Something else was feeding into my frustration, though, because as I watched John hurtle ever higher upwards, my career felt stagnant once again. After the high points of recent years – *Song & Dance, Guys & Dolls, Adrian Mole* – Marian and I still hadn't sat down, taken stock and made a plan. Instead of slowing up and letting everything consolidate, we'd pushed on as we always had. But there was one role in particular which had become a source of increasing tension between us: Peter Pan – the boy who never grew up being played by the woman who was also stuck in time in many ways too.

I'd first done the play in 1972 at the Manchester Opera House and then at the Palladium opposite Ron Moody in 1975. I was young, small and it made sense. Great actresses including Maggie Smith had appeared in *Peter Pan*. But in late 1987, after doing *The Mystery of Edwin Drood* at the Savoy Theatre, I started performing the role again – this time with a twist. The production was *Peter Pan: the Musical* and George Cole would play Captain Hook. The following year, I did the part again opposite both Eric Sykes and on a national tour with Christopher Timothy.

It was one thing flying above stages when I was in my early twenties, but another now I was forty. Pan was a physically demanding role and also felt more and more like Groundhog Day. I was tired and uninspired by work that might be paying the bills, but felt like it was eroding my credibility again. And with memories of the rerelease of 'Shout' still lingering, I became more and more frustrated with Marian and aware of how differently we were starting to see things. She was still in variety 'show business' and flinging-anything-that-might-stick mode. What had motivated me to get up and out of Glasgow, though, was the possibility of growing beyond what was around me as a child. I had always craved change. Now *Peter Pan* felt lazy and I became increasingly critical of the offers Marian came with.

'I can't.'

'I won't.'

'Have you got any other ideas?'

I was pushing Marian to think differently. What I didn't realise was that she might have been unhappy too. But then, during a conversation like the ones we'd had every day for twenty-five years, Marian said something which took my breath away.

'I don't think this is working,' she said. 'You don't want to do anything I suggest.'

'Because it's all the same Marian!' I replied. 'I'm bored. I'm tired. And it's hard performing and looking enthusiastic when I feel like that.'

For me, it was just an ordinary conversation, the kind we'd been having more of lately but would work our way through. Even though I was dissatisfied, I never dreamed I might be better off with a new manager. Marian wasn't just a colleague. She was both my business partner and my second mother. But then I realised she meant what she said.

'I think perhaps it's time for us to split,' Marian continued.

Sometimes in life, you know in a split second that you can't go back. This was one of those moments. Time slowed, my mind rushed to keep up. Marian had been thinking about this. She wasn't just reacting in anger. She really did think it was best for us to stop working together.

'It's probably time for me to retire,' she continued. 'Janey hasn't been well. She needs someone to look after her. And I'd like to slow down a bit.'

A wave of panic rolled over me. But another part of me knew that Marian was only saying what had also begun to feel inevitable however much I'd tried to ignore it. We'd been together for so long and the recording industry was changing. It was no longer enough just to sing. MTV had launched, music videos were increasingly important, as were big arena shows. We'd had a great run, but sometimes you have to know when you've gone as far as you can together.

'Okay,' I said finally. 'If you think it's for the best.'

'I'll be here if you need me,' Marian said.

And in one short, totally unexpected conversation, one of the most stable relationships I'd ever had was over. In the weeks and months that followed, I felt as if I was floating and the person who had always tethered me to the ground had gone. I'd dial Marian's number without thinking before remembering what had happened and putting the phone down. I'd wonder what she'd think of an offer before realising I'd never know. I thought of her constantly and missed the partnership we'd shared since the moment I started out. Marian's loss felt huge and my grief only fed my insecurity with John. But the needier I became, the more he pulled away. John was in flight, I was in pursuit, and neither of us had ever learned, or made time, to communicate properly about our feelings.

I became clingy and demanding; John focused on work and became dismissive. Or at least it felt like that to me. And however much I tried to provoke him into engaging, he wasn't going to be pulled down into the fight. I zeroed in on the hope of fixing things by getting pregnant again, eating special foods, trying to centre myself through meditation – not realising that none of it would work until I started being honest with myself.

There's an Indian proverb which reminds me of that time. It's about a man who lives in a village and, one day, someone runs down the street shouting that a herd of elephants is running amok. But while all the other villagers start rushing away from the danger, going inside and closing their doors, the man refuses to.

'I have been a good person and lived a disciplined, spiritual life,' he thinks to himself. 'God will look after me.'

A neighbour urges the man to leave, to come with the rest of his friends who are fleeing.

'Take cover,' the neighbour calls.

But the man ignores him.

'The elephants are coming,' says a second neighbour, urging the man to leave.

But still he refuses.

'God will take care of me,' he thinks. 'I have done everything I needed to.'

But, of course, the elephants arrive at the village, stampede straight over the man and kill him.

'Why didn't you take care of me?' he says angrily when he gets to the afterlife and meets God. 'I lived a dutiful life, a spiritual life.'

'I did look after you,' God replies. 'In fact, I sent you two very loud messages from your neighbours. But you did not listen.'

And as things with John spiralled downwards, I wasn't listening either.

# 52

# Must You Go?

John was opening a salon in New York and, along with the American launch of his products, needed to move there for a while. So, in 1990, we went to New York to find an apartment and a school for Jordan. He was thirteen and didn't need any persuading, while I could fly back for work. A change would be good for us all. We rented a place in Manhattan and started exploring.

But, as the weeks passed, John became more and more withdrawn and, when Jordan went to stay with friends for a few days, he turned to me one evening with a serious look on his face.

'We need to speak,' John said. 'It's over.'

I looked at him. What did he mean?

'I can't do this anymore,' John continued.

I knew we weren't getting along, but had never, ever, considered for a moment that we'd split up. For me, this relationship was for a lifetime. And now he was ending it? I could hardly hear what John was saying. And being the kind of man who used his words carefully and never let just anything tumble out, he took his time explaining his decision. I didn't hear much of it. If my split with Marian had felt shocking, this was brutal.

'I know what I want in my life and where I'm going,' John said. 'I've been thinking about this for a while.'

I tried desperately to think clearly, say something to convince him he was making a mistake.

'Surely we can work this out?' I whispered. 'See a counsellor. Talk it through.'

'No. We've got nothing in common. We never did.'

I stared at John in shock. Where was all this coming from? If we really had nothing in common then how had we spent the last thirteen years talking non-stop? But people can surprise you when they are pushed into a corner, even when you've known them for years. The single-minded determination I'd so admired in my husband was now being turned on me and I hardly recognised this stranger as he dismantled our life with every syllable.

We got into bed that night, just as we had for so many years, but this time in silence. My body felt rigid, empty and afraid. I lay awake all night staring up at the ceiling as the lights of Manhattan flickered across it and a voice whispered at the back of my mind.

'So this is how Maurice felt all those years ago.'

When we got up the next morning, John suggested we go to my favourite place on Madison Avenue for breakfast. But as I watched him eat, I couldn't swallow. My stomach churned as I looked around the restaurant, another ordinary day for the people around us while life as I knew it was ending. Then John looked at me with a determined expression.

'We need to talk about Jordan,' he said.

John seemed to think the plans we'd made for Jordan to start school in America still stood and I should stay in the US too. He kept talking about Jordan again and again, but I could hardly think straight or string a sentence together. Jordan would be better off in America, John said. It was such a great opportunity for him. Surely I should agree to let our son stay to give him the best possible education? He was excited about the plan after all. It felt like I was outside my body as I forced myself to go through the motions, as if I was floating in a vacuum. And feisty as I could be in some situations, I suddenly disintegrated in the face of John's certainty.

Nothing comes close to the devastation you experience when life explodes so abruptly. At the time, John's attitude felt coldly calculated. He had it all planned out. And it took time for me to understand that he behaved as he did because he believed our relationship had run its course and he needed to stop us drawing out the agony any longer. We'd never learned how to be honest with each other either. As a small child, John had had a long hospital stay and been separated from his parents, and I think he'd learned to shut his emotions down then. And Betty and Eddie had hardly been models of healthy communication for me. Now, in the ruins of our marriage, we couldn't find a way to talk properly.

A week later, I flew back to London with Jordan after telling John I needed to think. But he continued to phone me daily, pressing me to decide about Jordan's future.

'I just don't know,' I kept saying as we talked. 'I can't decide.'

'But by not making a clear decision, you are going to ruin this opportunity,' John would say.

I felt so confused. Maybe John was right. Jordan was a teen-ager and I'd agreed to go to America in the first place because I thought it would help him discover a new world and perspec-tive. I'd had that kind of chance when I was his age. I didn't want to deny it to my son. And how would Jordan feel if I refused and separated him from his father?

But I also knew I couldn't live in America full-time now on my own. I had no support structure, professionally or personally. Plus, I was hoping that somehow this was all a blip and John would come to his senses. He felt like a differ-ent person, almost fevered, running on the adrenalin of his ambition and business goals. He was no longer the man I'd spent years with and if we descended into arguments and fights over Jordan, I feared it would only push us further apart – and I knew what that could do to a child. John kept talking about a separation. We weren't divorcing. I wouldn't lose Jordan forever. We could talk on the phone every day. I could fly over. If breaking apart was what I needed to do in order to get our family back together then I'd do it. However painful it was.

In late September, I flew back to the US with Jordan so that he could start at the school we'd found for him. It was the kind of place you read about in books – every subject, every facility, extensive grounds. It was the best of the best. Clinging on to the fantasy that John just needed some time to realise this was all a mistake, I even helped find the two of them a house to rent. John's sister and her four children were moving over, so I knew Jordan would have family around him.

'I need to go back to London for work,' I said to him when it was all finally settled. 'But I'll be back soon. We'll see each other all the time and Dad will be here.'

Jordan trusted what I said and, yet again, I played my part perfectly: keep smiling, agree to it all, keep things peaceful, play nice. I only fell apart when I got back to London; grieving the loss of my marriage, but, most of all, my son.

# 53

# Getting Well

'How do you feel?' the therapist asked.

It was a few months after I'd got back from New York and, while there was press speculation about why John and I were living apart, we'd continued to maintain the fiction it was just because of work. But the fact we didn't tell Jordan the whole truth is something I've always regretted. We didn't spell out to him exactly what was happening and, as I clung to the idea my separation from John wouldn't last forever, I also avoided talking about it. Instead, I flew back and forth to America as much as I could when John was travelling for work, and 'treated' Jordan to weekends and holidays staying at hotels in Manhattan, going to see films, or eating pizza and ice cream. It felt unreal and was obviously very confusing for Jordan. Then, after seeing him, I'd either fly back to the UK or go to the Siddha Yoga ashram in upstate New York to study, read and meditate, which helped keep me grounded as I tried to create a new framework for my life.

How had I ended up living apart from my son and checking into hotels to see him? I just couldn't begin to understand how a life that had felt so secure had crumbled. I lost weight and withdrew personally from all but the people closest to me before painting on a smile in public, feeling utterly lost. And for the first time in my life, I couldn't find a way to bounce back.

I was sitting with a therapist in a rehabilitation clinic in Arizona. It was called The Meadows and had opened a few years before. When someone I respected told me they were doing good work there and advised me to try it, I agreed because I knew I had to do something to put myself back together and make sense of how the breakdown of my marriage to John had completely crushed me. I also did not dare to do anything like that in the UK in case the papers got hold of it. I needed to experience my grief in private.

But as I looked at the therapist now, I didn't know what to say.

How did I feel? I didn't know. I never really had. I'd just flung myself forwards my whole life. Talking about feelings was like asking me to speak in a language I'd never been taught. But over the next six weeks at The Meadows, a few things started to become clear. I realised, for instance, that I'd always felt different. Whether it was my parents and our life at home, or being so young when 'Shout' came out, a girl in the very male world of music, or a young woman who was convinced everyone else was doing drugs and having wild sex, I'd long felt separate. Less than. And, despite having success, I'd never got rid of that feeling.

I started to make sense of the impact of my childhood and see my part in the breakdown of my marriage. I believed I couldn't live without love. I had gone from home to having Marian, to marriage with Maurice and John. I had never been alone and the prospect of life on my own scared me. That's why I had hung on and clung on, knowing things weren't right with John – and Marian too – but desperate to ignore the truth and trying to keep things 'perfect'.

It felt like a relief to start unpicking it all, and being with people whose stories were different to mine, but who shared so many similar feelings, also helped. Many of us believe we are unique, but our pain rarely is. It's just part of being human.

Most of all, the exhausting responsibility I'd carried for so long was suddenly lifted as people looked after me. I'd spent a lifetime caring for other people, putting their needs before my own, believing that if I was 'good' enough to be loved, I'd be fixed. In many ways, I was just an outline of a person who'd never learned how to be whole and happy. All I'd done was perform.

That, of course, was the theory. Now I had to put it all into practice. But heartbreak isn't fixed in a few weeks and neither are the emotional habits of a lifetime. I had been lucky enough to have the money and time to get on a fast-track to finally begin the healing process. My time at The Meadows had given me some new tools. Meditation and its allied disciplines provided others. And when I got back to the UK, I certainly felt like I could face the world again. If one part of me had died, another now felt reborn. After all the confusion of my relationships with both Marian and John ending, I could look forwards and start to embrace becoming independent, trusting my judgement and making my own decisions from a whole new perspective.

But there was only one way I knew how to do all this: by reconnecting with music. Take away the industry politics, the execs, the highs and lows of success and fame, and music had nourished me ever since I was a child.

It was time to get back to business.

# VII

# 54

# Billy Won't Let Me Off the Hook

For so many years, my brother had talked about my musical instincts.

'You know a hit when you hear it,' Billy would tell me during all the years with Marian as he urged me to refocus on music. 'You knew "Shout" had something right at the start. "To Sir" and "Oh Me Oh My" too. You also know how to make a melody sound good, often better than when first presented. You've got to trust yourself.'

Billy had been working in the music industry for years by now. After doing promotions when he first got to London and songwriting with Maurice, he'd got into A&R before co-founding a music publishing company with Laurence Ronson. Billy had the experience, but I also trusted him completely. I knew my brother was the right person to help me get back into music on my own terms.

'We're going to have to work hard,' Billy said as we sat together.

I was now living in the house John and I had bought after moving out of the flat Betty had disliked so much, and it was the first time I'd lived alone. While I saw my parents, Billy and

Edwina a lot, I still felt like I was rattling around when I wasn't working (which was most of the time). But I wasn't going to feel sorry for myself. Billy and I agreed I'd been out of the recording business for a few years, which was a long time in an industry that moved so fast, and now we'd have to find the right material for me to work on.

'You're also going to have to write some of it,' Billy told me and the familiar wave of panic filled me – the old fear of making mistakes and admitting the messy truth of who I was, plus thoughts of Lennon, McCartney, Elton John and the Gibb brothers. If my own insecurities weren't enough to stun me into silence, thinking of that lot certainly was.

But I also knew it was time for change.

'I'm managing a young guy who I think you won't feel intimidated by,' Billy said. 'The two of you should meet, talk and we'll see what happens.'

Soon a young songwriter called Steve DuBerry had come to see me and we talked about the kind of material I was drawn to. Two albums in particular had sustained me over the past couple of years, pieces of work with an emotional rawness that resonated. One was Don Henley's *The End of Innocence* with a lyric on a track called 'The Heart of the Matter' that I listened to again and again:

I think it's about forgiveness
Even if you don't love me anymore.

The other was Bonnie Raitt's *Luck of the Draw* and I'd played the album non-stop, particularly the song 'I Can't Make You Love

Me'. For obvious reasons. John and I were no longer together, but I still wasn't completely emotionally separated from him. In fact, I went round in circles for a long time hoping we'd somehow find a way back because it was hard to accept the marriage had been over for a while before John had said what he did.

To sift through it all, I'd leaned ever more into my practices of meditating and studying, staying at the Siddha Yoga ashram in upstate New York on trips to see Jordan. I'd also become more physically disciplined than I ever had been and given up drinking because before going to The Meadows, I'd been drowning my sorrows a little too often. I even started exercising seriously for the first time in my life after Jordan got on the school athletics team and told me he thought I'd enjoy it. I decided to try it, if only to make him laugh when I told him, before realising my son was right. I'd always been high energy, but getting outside and into nature cleared the fog in my brain and I was soon running six miles a day.

Two weeks after Steve and I talked, he came back with an almost finished melody which we tweaked until we were all happy.

'Now the lyrics,' Billy said after we'd listened. 'So what do you want to say?'

I looked at him.

'I don't know.'

But Billy wasn't going to let me off the hook.

'If you did know, what would it be?'

I loved that thought, but also felt agitated that I didn't have a quick comeback. I sat for a moment and let it sink in.

'I'm just a bit worn out,' I said finally, 'I don't want to fight anymore.'

'There's yer title.'

I smiled as I realised that the right words were inside me. We had a title. Now it was time to write the story. Billy and I sat together as we found more words – I sung them over the melody and made them knit together. It happened instantly, and after a few days, we were confident that we had a really good song. Now we had to find enough others to put together an album and get me a new record deal. Maybe 'I Don't Wanna Fight' could be on it.

# 55

# Four Hours of Waiting

*B*illy and I sat in the record company office waiting to see the exec. He was the son of someone I'd worked with a lot during my career, so I'd known him since he was a child. I was hoping we could shortcut some of the small talk and properly discuss what I was hoping to do. But we'd been here for about twenty minutes and there was no sign of him. I looked at Billy nervously. If getting my 'Shout' deal at Decca had happened quickly, it was clearly going to be more difficult this time around.

'They've got to see you're serious,' Billy had said to me when we started talking about going to see songwriters, publishers and labels.

When, once, people would have come to my manager or producer, I was now going to have to be far more hands-on. There was no room for ego or clinging on to the past. Billy and I knew the execs would be confused by all the mixed messages I'd given during my career, all the different forms of work and styles of music. They couldn't be sure of who I was. And, musically speaking, I was coming back from the dead after years away from the charts. But I was used to making changes and surviving; I'd always been willing to experiment. Dusty had once told me I was brave *because of it and I was prepared now to do whatever it took. My marriage was over, my son was in America, my time was all mine and so I should at the very least do something with it.*

*'They just need to see you,' Billy had said. 'And hear you. Then they'll really get it. Your voice is as good as it always was. Maybe even better.'*

*The minutes ticked by as Billy and I sat waiting. Half an hour passed. A secretary gave us soothing smiles from behind a desk every now and again. We knew the guy was in his office. What was the hold up? When the phone finally rang, the secretary looked at us with an embarrassed smile.*

*'Something's come up,' she said. 'He can't see you.'*

*At first, I felt hurt. Then I felt angry. I'd known this guy since he was running around in nappies. And now he thought I was so past it that basic manners didn't even apply?*

*'What is he on?' was my first thought.*

*Fuck him, my second.*

# 56

# Dance Floor Diva

Music had changed a lot. Apart from all the new technology, the influence of DJs and dance remixes were all-powerful in the early Nineties. With my new label, I was going to embrace it all.

It had taken a year to get a deal, but Peter Robinson, a great A&R man, had just founded a label called Dome and wanted to sign me because, just like the execs all those years before, he believed in my voice. Billy and I had worked hard to find the right tracks to record and then Peter had come on board with new ideas and material. No flimsy pop this time. The new album would play to my strengths by combining soulful ballads with upbeat tracks mixed by some of the best DJs and producers.

We did mix after mix of each song, trying to get the sound right, but one song, and one mix in particular, stood out: a track called 'Independence' which Brothers in Rhythm transformed into a high-energy dance track with a strong bassline and overlaid horns. As we counted down to releasing it as the first single from my new album, Dome had sent out hundreds of advance copies to DJs to get their response.

'I thought she died years ago – but a hit,' one wrote.

I was getting a lot of that these days because music was, and still is, an industry built on youth, and midlife women, particularly ones who'd been around so long people felt they were ancient, didn't usually get back into the charts after years away from them. 'Battle of the wrinklies,' one headline shouted as it pitted my upcoming release against another female artist. I was only forty-four.

You can, however, feel it when the right momentum is building. With Peter and the Dome team behind me, I was delighted when Tony King, who'd started out in the Sixties in promotions before working with everyone from the Rolling Stones to Ringo and John, agreed to manage me. I'd known him for decades and he was a respected industry figure, a real tastemaker, and I was lucky to have him.

'I love your new material,' Tony had said when we first met. 'And if there was any of some of the old stuff you recorded, I wouldn't be able to do this.'

Fair point.

'Now people need to get to know you as a great singer again. We've got to show you aren't stuck in the past and have changed with the times. And your new look has to be streamlined, simplified; less is more.'

I was ready for change. More than two years on from my separation, I was going through a metamorphosis, which was painful but also necessary. Together with Tony, we worked on my image, the video, marketing and promotion and, by the time 'Independence' was released, I was ready. My hair was shorter, my clothes more muted, but, more importantly, I was doing the right material that I connected with and also had an army behind me now. Plus, crucially, it all added up to a well-planned strategy.

I'd be lying, though, if I said I flipped back into the industry without a second thought. It was nerve-wracking almost three decades on from 'Shout' to be back doing PAs in places like the Ministry of Sound. A lot of the crowd hadn't even been born when I was first around. Sobering to say the least. But I was also back in the one place I'd always felt comfortable: on a stage, entertaining people, using all my experience to connect to them and feel that familiar energy lifting me.

I knew many people would interpret the lyrics of 'Independence' as a comment on my marriage and assume I was saying I'd ended it because I wanted to be out on my own. Little did they know. The lyrics and energy of 'Independence' resonated with me for precisely the opposite reason: I'd been forced to discover my autonomy; now I was determined to use my anger about it positively. One community in particular took the track to their hearts. 'Independence' was an anthem to strength and was rapidly adopted by the queer community who embraced me so wholeheartedly, I will be forever grateful.

I knew this time that if this didn't work, I wasn't going to fall apart. I couldn't pin my new sense of self on to a chart comeback. And I knew more than most that a lot of it was just the luck of the draw. I'd tried new things in the past like the Atlantic material and, however good it was, it hadn't stuck. I had to be aware, as usual, that I couldn't be crushed if 'Independence' didn't work.

But however Zen I tried to be, I was thrilled when it entered the charts at number fourteen in January 1993 before climbing to number eleven. The press was all over my return to music – and so too were music critics, some of whom were snarky, but many approving. 'Independence' got to number one on the dance charts and to number three on the Dance Club Play Billboard chart in the US. The response was overwhelming and even the odd furious newspaper letter writer advising me to 'collect my pension' or declaring that I was 'a has-been' couldn't pull me down.

I'd also learned that good things tend to create more of the same, and Billy and I soon had another reason to celebrate. Tina Turner, who'd made a movie about her life, had heard 'I Don't Wanna Fight' and recorded it for the soundtrack. We had Steve DuBerry to thank because he'd taken the song to his friend Sade who – like Tina – was managed by Roger Davies, She played it to Roger who took it to Tina and 'I Don't Wanna Fight' was released as a single in 1993. It became a worldwide hit reaching number nine on the US Billboard charts and number seven in the UK a few months after 'Independence'.

People have often asked since why I didn't keep the track for myself, but my response is this: it was Tina Turner. She was an icon and, from my own experience, I knew how enormous the promotional machine behind her would be. That doesn't hurt. Plus, parts of Tina's story felt familiar to me. She had enjoyed early success before her career dipped and she ended up doing TV work and cabaret shows. Then she'd released *Private Dancer* and her career had exploded again in this country. Having my work in her orbit felt like a huge affirmation and I got my second Grammy nomination the following year. The fact that it was for songwriting made it even sweeter. After all the years of doubt, I was finally creating music that wasn't just right for my voice, but also for other artists. And I had done it by starting to put myself in the song.

Suddenly, life was like it had been in the early days again: a whirl of performances and the release of follow-up singles including a track Barry Gibb had written for me. I flew over to Miami to work with him on *Let Me Wake Up In Your Arms* and being in the studio with Barry had felt like coming full circle. I also went on the road again to promote the album, Jordan spent the summer with me and it felt like life was knitting back together again. My return to music had been all – and more than – I'd hoped for.

But then came a call that would spin things in a completely new – and unexpected – direction. I was in Cornwall with Tony preparing to perform at a Radio One Roadshow when he told me Peter had phoned.

'He's very excited,' Tony said. 'Nigel Martin-Smith wants you to guest vocal with his new band.'

'You mean Take That?' I asked in surprise.

'Yes.'

I knew Take That, of course. A year before, they'd had their first hit with a cover of 'It Only Takes a Minute' and followed it up with a string of Top Ten singles before 'Pray' got to number one. They were exploding. And, of course, I'd always liked to do things that surprised people. But David Bowie was one thing, collaborating with the biggest – and very young – pop stars of the moment was another. They didn't look much older than Jordan. And he was fifteen. I wasn't convinced.

'What's the song?'

'"Relight My Fire",' Tony replied.

It was a disco track that Dan Hartman had written and had a hit with in the Seventies featuring an incredible vocal from Loleatta Holloway.

'And they want me to do what she did?' I asked Tony.

'No. They want you to sound like you. They love the album. They want to work with you.'

I stared at Tony. I wasn't quite sure what to say. It was flattering, of course, to even be asked. But it had taken three years of hard work to reinvent myself. And did I really want to risk all that by singing with a boy band?

# VIII

# 57

# Relight My Fire

Flames shot out of iron bowls on a stage flooded in red, yellow and white light as the music started and Gary, Robbie, Howard, Mark and Jason – shirtless under pin-striped waistcoats or wearing black jackets and baggy trousers – started dancing. Screams peppered the *Top of the Pops* audience as I stood hidden behind a curtain in a plum velvet jacket waiting for the moment when the boys would group together, hold their hands high and I'd walk onto stage to belt out my lines. It was October 1993 and 'Relight My Fire' had gone straight to number one. Twenty-nine years after 'Shout' debuted, I'd topped the charts for the first time a month before my forty-fifth birthday.

It had taken some persuasion to get me there. I just couldn't shake off the feeling that I might end up looking slightly ridiculous, a middle-aged woman hanging on to boys young enough to be my sons. Robbie was only nineteen – just four years older than Jordan – and even Howard, the oldest member of the band, was only twenty-five.

'Just try out the vocal,' Take That's manager Nigel Martin-Smith had said as we discussed the project. 'And if you don't like it, it won't go out.'

After going to a studio to lay down my vocals with Gary Barlow, I left knowing he was a great singer and musician. And Nigel, my team and the record label were all so ecstatic about the track that I decided to put my fears aside. The true turning point came, however, when we shot the video at the Ministry of Sound because from the moment I arrived, it was clear Take That weren't just a bunch of kids having fun, but disciplined and focused. Plus, they were incredibly welcoming and insisted I have their trailer within five minutes. That kind of warmth put me completely at ease and set the pattern for a relationship that's lasted more than thirty years.

I think my doubts were partly about my own insecurities, but also because I'd bought into the idea that bands need to be forged in the fires of school days, playing in their bedrooms and clawing their way up. Some of the greats do it that way, of course, but the idea that boy bands are somehow less worthy minimises the innate talent of the best ones like Take That. Success in the music industry can certainly be arbitrary. Some of the best vocalists and musicians I've ever worked with are complete unknowns. But few people get to the top, and stay there, without a fierce determination – and an incredible work ethic.

Luck is also involved. And timing. Sometimes, music just hits at the right moment, and the decision to do 'Relight My Fire' was clever. First, it was being played a lot on the club scene; second, it was a great piece of disco music; and third, pairing me with the band sparked something. Having come up in gay clubs, Take That now had a new audience of teenage girl fans and were crossing over into the mainstream. But while the record label had initially wanted a singer who was known in dance music, Nigel and the boys had championed me. The late Eighties had seen some iconic partnerships between male artists and older female ones – including George Michael and Aretha Franklin, plus Dusty and the Pet Shop Boys. Now, 'Relight My Fire' would evolve the idea for the Nineties: a hot – and very young – boy band teaming up with an artist who'd been around for decades. The song, the imagery and Take That's upward momentum, plus a dash of my legacy, all came together and 'Relight My Fire' was a huge hit.

Soon, Nigel approached me with the next idea: he wanted me to join the boys on a big UK and European tour. But, once again, I had my doubts. The record had worked, but would their fans really want to see me on stage? Nigel suggested I go to see the boys live, just to understand what performing with them might look like, and it took about ten seconds to realise I'd be crazy to pass up the opportunity. Being on stage, performing and connecting to an audience had always been the most precious part of my work and this was a chance to play to a new, younger audience of thousands.

Take That was riding the cusp of a wave and I could be part of it. It was time to go on the road again.

# 58

# Reborn, Reignited and Rediscovered

Remember the battered vans I'd travelled in when I started out as a pop star? This time around, things were very different. Being on the road now was a series of luxury buses, private planes and hotels, swept up in the kind of band mania I'd seen in the Sixties. The Beatles. The Monkees. The Beach Boys. Now Take That were inspiring fan hysteria as we travelled city to city across the UK and Europe.

After I opened the show, the boys came on for the main event before I joined them again for the last song. 'Relight My Fire' was the apex of a show with next-level production values. As the boys disappeared for a costume change, dozens of dancers climbed out from under the stage in red devil outfits, writhing as the music built, before I appeared dressed in a skintight see-through red lace dress wearing an incredible wig styled into a bright red – and very backcombed – mullet.

After performing a few lines of theatrical verse, I finished with a cackle of 'evil' laughter and shouted 'Feed the fire' as flames roared up at the edges of the stage. And then the boys were lifted from below on a platform, framed in silhouette against the spotlights, dressed in new, and outrageous, outfits. Jason in a red rope 'kilt' with black shorts underneath; Howard in a black leather jock strap, bare buttocks and red satin chaps; Robbie in a red and white satin boxer's robe, boots and shorts; Gary in a red suit with a black polo neck; and Mark in red trousers and a cape. All of them wearing devil horns. It was over the top, camp and fun.

As the boys sang and danced, I reclined on the stairs behind them with a disdainful look on my face before walking down to sing. And then the five of them surrounded me before lifting me high into the air above their shoulders as the track finished with an explosion of fireworks.

The crowds went wild. Every time. And if that's not a one-way ticket to reigniting your vitality and youth after the crushing rejection of a marriage breakdown, I don't know what is.

The next few months were a heady succession of cities and stages, roaring crowds and dancing into the early hours with the boys in nightclubs because there was no way I could come off stage after all that and go to bed. The feeling of euphoria was just too powerful and, wherever the band went, you could feel the temperature shoot up in whatever bar or club they entered. I felt lucky to be so generously wrapped up in their success, morphing into a cross between one of the boys, a mother hen and an object of desire on stage. Soon, they'd nicknamed me 'Loobylu' and then just 'Looby' as we moved from city to city to perform.

'Are you coming for a drink Looby?'

'What were the Sixties like Looby?'

'Oh Looby's meditating again.'

It was during those months on tour that I really got to know them all. They were young, hurling themselves into the chances they'd created, and I understood how that felt. Gary was curious about everything, incredibly funny and filled with ambition. He was also fascinated by antiques, so we loved to shop together in whatever city we were in. Robbie, the baby of the band, was like a jumping bean, and would often come to my dressing room to show me lyrics he'd written. He seemed almost unsure about them, but it was clear he was a natural songwriter. Howard was sweet, reserved and the big brother to them all, while Mark was incredibly warm, relaxed and also interested in meditation. In fact, by the end of the tour, I had them all trying it.

Jason was the one I got into deep conversations with and we'd talk about anything from philosophical beliefs to how the world was changing and the books we were reading. A lot of rubbish was written at the start about us being in a relationship. Honestly? We'd laugh because it was so ridiculous. I had a great friendship with all of the boys and the attention they gave me was a huge boost to my confidence, but no more than that.

It was a heady, exciting time with a great group of people and that kind of experience creates a feeling of camaraderie, family even. I still think fondly of those early days with Take That. They've grown older, had families of their own, some are still performing and others have retreated from the spotlight. But we shared some extraordinary moments together and, while the 'Shout' days had been a mix of massive highs, punctured with insecurity and loneliness, this time around was pure, joyful adrenaline for me. I wasn't carrying the whole performance, I was just there for a small piece of it and, for perhaps the first time, I really allowed myself to soak in the applause. For so many years, I'd either rushed quickly off stage or stood there feeling as if I'd somehow kidded everyone with a performance that wasn't as good as they thought it was. Now, I finally allowed myself to enjoy the crowd's reaction and it was wonderful.

And if any of it risked going to my head, I was soon cut down to size. Jordan came to see the show and didn't know quite what to make of his mother up there with the boy band of the moment. And Betty?

'How can you put one foot in front of the other in a dress like that?' she cried. 'Are you sure it won't rip? There's enough bare flesh up there without you revealing all.'

# 59

# Time to Make Amends

When Jordan told me he wanted to come back to England, I couldn't have been happier. We'd seen each other regularly while he was living in the US, but it wasn't the same as living together and the day-to-day experience of making meals, chatting over cups of tea and doing all the 'boring' stuff like sports, homework and lifts. But now Jordan had decided that he wanted to come back to the UK to sit his A levels and go to university here too.

'I want to come home,' he'd said when he called to tell me.

Five years had felt like a long time and, anxious to convince my now seventeen-year-old son to spend as much time at home as possible, I sold the small house where I'd been living since my split with John and bought a larger place nearby to make sure we had enough space for all Jordan's friends. He started at a new school, reconnected with the kids he'd grown up with and I made sure my door was always open, whatever the time, if he wanted to chat when he came in from a night out, just as Janey and Alf had done for me all those years before. Jordan had missed a lot of things while he was in the US and, while cricket was top of the list, I wasn't far behind.

But it was also time to make amends because being with Jordan again meant I had to reckon with some of my behaviour. I felt guilty about so many things: the years we'd spent apart, not telling him the truth about me and John for so long, and not being present enough when he was very young because I was working so much. Now, with him home, we could finally – and fully – talk it all over and I apologised to Jordan for all the things I'd got wrong. He talked to me too about his feelings, and this kind of honesty and vulnerability brought us closer together.

No one ever said that becoming more aware of yourself – the good bits as well as the bad – is easy. I have had to forgive myself again and again about many things, and I'm still not completely there about Jordan. Those years left a mark, not just on me, but on all three of us. None of us got away pain free. John and Jordan suffered too. But I tell myself I did the best I could at the time and have to trust that the path we each took individually was the one we were meant to follow.

I was also lucky enough to have a son who never held on to anger. I loved having Jordan home and, even when he left it, we remained close. He's gone on to build a very successful career far away from the industries John and I are in, as well as a happy family life. So while John and I certainly made mistakes, we have a son wise and loving enough to forgive them.

# 60

# Champagne for Lulu

Back when I was doing *Guys & Dolls*, Richard Eyre had introduced me to a group of young comedians he knew and one of them was Jennifer Saunders. Within a few years, she and Dawn French were household names and, when Jennifer had another hit with *Absolutely Fabulous*, she called to ask me to do a cameo, playing a version of myself in Eddie and Patsy's crazy universe. I happily agreed.

The episode was called 'New Best Friend' and saw Eddie and Patsy fall out over an old friend's visit to see Eddie who was expecting to party with her. Instead, Bettina – who was played by Miranda Richardson – was no fun anymore because she'd had a baby. But while Eddie was anxious to start the party again with her original best friend, Patsy was still annoyed and the two ended up sitting at opposite ends of Joe's Café trying to 'out friend' each other. Patsy had strong-armed her way on to a table with Zandra Rhodes and Britt Ekland, while poor Eddie sat alone until I walked past and she dragged me to her table.

'What do you want?' I hissed before getting up to walk away.

'I may well have a gun in my bag,' Eddie said as she grabbed me. 'I'll shoot you and then try very hard to turn it on myself if you leave, alright?'

I reluctantly sat back down after Eddie promised to pay for lunch before listing all the many dishes I wanted to order in revenge. And then Jennifer clicked her fingers and cried 'Champagne for Lulu', desperate to keep me happy – and also to let the rest of the restaurant know we were having lunch together. The line would get repeated every time I appeared in *Ab Fab* and became an affectionate send-up of my slightly waspish version of 'Lulu'. The end of 'New Best Friend', for instance, saw me licking my dessert plate as Eddie asked me who did my PR.

'You do,' I replied before leaving with Britt Ekland.

The next year, both Jennifer and Dawn asked me to do a sketch for a new series of their comedy show and I knew that, just like Kenny, they wouldn't want me to passively sit by but take part in the skit and send myself up. I was more than happy to oblige as the stunt coordinator strapped me into a vest fitted with pellets of stage blood that would be triggered when they 'shot' me.

It was a take-off of *Pulp Fiction* and I was playing hostage to Jennifer and Dawn's captors, dressed *Pulp Fiction*-style in black suits and white shirts, channelling John Travolta and Samuel L. Jackson energy. But instead of keeping quiet, I kept bursting into 'Shout' until they got so tired of it, they pumped 'bullets' into me. All I needed to do as I sat in a white shirt, on a white sofa, in a white room, was keep my arms away from my body to allow the fake blood pellets to safely explode. Instead, I instinctively clamped my arms to my sides as 'blood' exploded all over my body and the wall behind me. When the cameras cut, I realised I was in agony because one of the pellets had buried itself in my arm.

'I think I've been shot,' I said weakly when the cameras stopped rolling and I looked down to see very real blood soaking my shirt.

The BBC crew looked at each other nervously. The director went white. The producer Jon Plowman rapidly gathered me up and took me to A&E looking like I'd been caught in a gun fight. After being patched up, we finished the scene the next day and, soon after, a package arrived for me at home. Inside was a tiny silver heart from Penhaligon's with the inscription 'We shot Lulu' on one side and 'sorry' on the other. Dawn and Jennifer certainly know how to make me smile.

# 61

# Lunch with Elton

*T*he thing I've always loved about friendships is that they can develop out of the blue: a stranger walks into your life, there's a click and a bond is quickly forged. But, at other times, you can suddenly become close to someone you've known for years. That's what happened with me and Elton John.

It started when John Reid invited me and Take That to his house for lunch with him and Elton while we were touring. I'd always liked Elton and admired his career, of course. But, over lunch, we got chatting about songwriting because after putting it off for so long, I was keen to do more of it now that Billy and I had got into a rhythm. By the time lunch was finished, Elton had offered to write with me. I think he liked the fact that I just kept hurling myself back into music, still passionate about it, even after all these years, and refusing to be beaten.

The idea of working with him was daunting, but, after that lunch, I became close friends with both Elton and his then part-ner, now husband, David, who I also clicked with. The two of them were endlessly generous and outrageously fun. Then, in 1995, David was making the documentary Tantrums and Tiaras and decided he wanted to capture me and Elton at work.

*Me and Elton John forever on film?*

*Billy and I wrote feverishly, trying to come up with some lyrics that would channel even a fraction of the Bernie Taupin magic. Because while most songs are created music first, lyrics second, Elton and Bernie had always inverted the process. Bernie wrote the words and then Elton somehow created a melody that fitted them perfectly. I'd always known he worked quickly, but, after arriving at the studio with a pile of my lyrics, Elton had taken a quick look, sat down at the piano at 4pm and was done by 4.30pm. We had a cup of tea and were back at the piano singing the song by 5pm. I just about managed to get my voice to cooperate.*

*But, over those years, my friendship with both Elton and David was cemented as Billy and I continued to write together and artists I admired including Bonnie Raitt, Wynonna Judd and Cher picked up songs we'd done. Elton played a big part in encouraging me to believe in myself, and I will be forever grateful. Some artists think they are so far above all the rest, they pull up the ladder behind them. But Elton? He'll be the one holding on to it, lifting you up and probably making outrageous jokes as he does it. Elton and David have championed and supported me for more than thirty years now, and both are family to me. I adore them and their boys.*

# 62

# Weeks, Not Months

You know by your late forties that your parents won't live forever, but, somehow, never think you'll actually lose them. Or, how acutely painful the hole it creates in your life will be when you do. But, in March 1996, Edwina called me late at night.

'There's something wrong with Mum,' she said. 'Her stomach is swollen. She looks awful.'

The previous year, Betty had had a bladder operation and, although I'd offered to pay for it privately, she'd insisted she wanted it on the NHS. Now divorced from John, and having realised I'd taken a lot for granted financially in the past, I was no longer spending as I once had. And, just as she had during those Bond Street shopping days years before, Betty didn't want me spending my money on her. However much I insisted, she refused to let me pay for a private operation.

After speaking to Edwina, though, I was worried that Mum might have had some kind of delayed complication from the previous procedure and called my gynaecologist. The next day, Edwina picked up Betty, who arrived at the doctor's office looking fabulous because however religious she'd become, Mum had never quite conquered the 'sin' of vanity. Betty wasn't going to go out looking scruffy, even when she was feeling so ill. The doctor spent all day doing tests before I took Mum home exhausted to my house. A few days later, he called to say he had the test results and I left Betty to rest while I went and got them.

'Mrs Lawrie has advanced cancer,' the doctor said. 'I'm going to give you the name of an oncologist I know at the Royal Marsden who can advise on what treatment might be suitable.'

Another conversation that makes the ground beneath you shift forever.

'But how long do you think she has?' I asked.

'I would say weeks not months.'

A strange kind of stillness fills you when you hear words like that. I've noticed ever since in movies or on TV that people react in an instant when they are given bad news. But I felt frozen, almost disbelieving, as I tried to take it in. As anyone who's cared for someone who is terminally ill knows, though, life instantly becomes a whirl of appointments and opinions, treatment options and chasing down doctors on the phone. We were all shocked that Betty was even ill – Eddie was the one who'd drunk and smoked his way through the past few decades while she hadn't even touched caffeine for years. However much we were hoping for a miracle, though, we quickly understood we wouldn't get one. The doctors said Betty could have some chemotherapy to slow the growth of the tumours that had started in her stomach, but nothing was going to stop the cancer.

Eddie was lost. So was Billy. The two of them could hardly take in what was happening and so Edwina, Gordon and I took charge. Gordon's wedding was a few months away and we knew it would give Mum a point to fix on. Despite the drugs, the side effects and the pain, she was determined to keep going.

There were no big conversations about the past. We'd never found the words for it and, by now, it also seemed like a lifetime ago anyway. But happy moments of childhood hovered in the air around us as Betty started to sing for me again for the first time in many years. And over the following weeks and months, there was one song in particular that she loved, 'Who Do You Know in Heaven (That Made You the Angel You Are)'. It was a classic crooner song that many people had done including Nat King Cole, and Betty had looked at me one day after singing it.

'You will always be blessed,' she said. 'You've looked after me so well and God will look after you too.'

Sometimes just one sentence encapsulates the weight – and love – of many years.

That summer, we all celebrated Gordon's wedding and Mum looked beautiful in a grey-blue dress as she danced with us and laughed, and we all felt hopeful we still had time together. A few weeks later, she insisted that Billy and I go to Los Angeles to do some songwriting we'd been putting off for a while, and that Edwina also go on a family holiday which had been postponed.

'You have to go,' she said when I went to see her in the flat we'd rented for my parents near Edwina in Blackheath. 'Your lives can't stop. I'll be here.'

But a week into the trip, I called home and Gordon said Mum was too tired to talk. The next day, she was the same and I knew we had to get back. Billy and I got on an overnight flight to London, Edwina started the journey home too, but, just after we landed, Gordon phoned.

'She died about twenty minutes ago,' he told me.

I think Betty knew we were all on the way back to her and wanted to spare us. She died with Gordon, her youngest child with whom she'd always shared a special bond. And as pain at losing my mother, the person I'd protected, parented, resented and loved in equal measure for so many years, filled me, the depth of the loss I felt took me by complete surprise. We were all lost. Mum had been the centre around which everything had spun for decades.

Grief is not something that disappears. You have to learn to live with it. But the next few months were hard and, soon, I was back in Los Angeles again writing with Billy. I'd always found Beverly Hills a bit unreal. It's so perfect, it's almost too much. Constant sunshine, beautiful people, wealth oozing out of every corner. But on one particular day while we were there, the city that was usually so manicured and polished had suddenly transformed when it started raining and grief washed over me.

'Lu?' Billy asked as we sat chatting on a veranda near the studio. 'Are you listening to anything I'm saying?'

I looked at my brother and then across the city skyline. It was sometimes hard to take in just how far Billy and I had travelled from where we'd come. Beverly Hills had no rough edges, nothing was out of place. And, as I looked at my brother, I remembered the tiny boy I'd protected back in Glasgow, the scabbed knees and grimy pavements, our flat packed with people and noise.

'Doesn't all this feel unreal to you sometimes?' I asked.

Billy and I started chatting and had soon captured our conversation in lyrics for a song that's still one of my proudest pieces of work. 'Where the Poor Boys Dance' is about ghosts, trying to find out who you are and needing to go back to the past to do it. Because however much I wanted to leave it all behind, Betty's death had sparked powerful feelings that still lay deep inside me. And however much I tried to wish them away, they weren't going anywhere.

# 63

# Eddie Finally Gets It

My father missed Betty terribly. But something incredible also happened a few months after she died because after years of alcohol abuse, Eddie simply gave up one day and never touched a drop again. I had never known a time when my father didn't drink, but they say you only stop when you are ready and Eddie clearly was. None of the rest of us, however, had any idea it was coming.

Jordan and I had taken Dad to New York for Christmas with John and his father. We'd had to surprise Eddie with the trip because otherwise he'd never have agreed to leave home – and the drink. But we were determined to get him away because he was so unhappy without Mum and so we got Dad into the car, drove him to Heathrow and one first-class lounge, plus a few drinks, later, and Eddie was relaxed enough to board the flight.

By now, John and I had been divorced for a few years and had found a way to not just coexist but start to be friends again. We both knew Christmas with his parents was important for Jordan, and John's father Isidore was also delighted. He was in a wheelchair by then and Eddie had watched as John carefully pushed

Isidore through the packed streets when we went out shopping on Fifth Avenue one day.

'He's a caring man Marie,' Dad said to me.

All these years on, my father was the only person who still used my original name and I knew he was right about John. Christmas, however, was tough in parts because Eddie was drinking heavily and, while I understood he was missing Mum, I also felt frustrated. We'd had so many years like this, and I looked forward to going to the ashram for a few days after Christmas because at least Eddie wouldn't be able to drink.

Everyone there knew Dad had recently lost his wife and made sure to be even more welcoming than usual when we arrived. But I was still surprised at how quickly Dad responded to this new, warm environment. He'd never been religious, and certainly gone nowhere near Mum's Mormonism, so I hadn't thought he'd really be interested. But as our days at the ashram settled into the set rhythm of meditation, yoga, chores and food, Dad responded to what was happening around him. It was a stimulating place after all, full of conversations and questions, and while Eddie hadn't been formally educated, he was intelligent and thoughtful. He told me he'd been sitting quietly in his room during meditations, thinking about things. For a man who'd never, ever, dug back into the past, it was a surprise to hear. But I'd always known my father had a pure heart. He'd told me that, even as a baby, I'd lean in and rest my head on his chest when he sang to me and I think it was because that was his true essence. Not the shame I could sense was still so powerfully inside him.

One day at lunch, a woman who was new to the ashram was firing questions at people, trying, as many do, to intellectualise a process that is beyond it, and Eddie looked at her.

'Excuse me lady,' he said. 'I hope you don't mind me saying but if you just sit and let it all soak in, everything's a process. You'll get your answers.'

In just a few days, my father had understood what it takes others a long, long time to realise. I was still worried, though, when I took Dad to the airport for his flight home. Eddie was going to fly alone because I had to stay in the US for work and I was nervous he'd get so drunk on the plane, he wouldn't be able to get off it. When I took him to the passenger lounge, we bumped into Jonathan Ross and his family.

'I'll look after Eddie,' Jonathan told me, but I wasn't sure whether it would be Dad or Jonathan who'd cause the most mischief on the flight home.

But when I called Dad to check he'd got back okay, he told me he hadn't touched a drop of alcohol.

'I just didn't want a drink,' Eddie said.

I couldn't quite believe it. My father had been drinking his whole life and, while I knew the ashram had done him some good, I didn't hold out any hope he'd carry on sober. He did though. Eddie stopped drinking for good from then on and I can't explain exactly what happened. I just know something profound shifted for my father. All the more remarkable is the fact that he remained sober even while he struggled with grief about losing Betty.

'I don't want to live anymore,' Dad would say now and again and we'd all try to pull him out of it.

'You don't mean that,' I'd tell him. 'Mum has only just gone. You can't leave us too.'

Eddie went on for two more years, but, in October 1998, he had a mild heart attack. And while the doctors told us he'd be out of hospital in a few days, he had another in the early hours of one morning and died. The power of the mind to will the body to give up is fierce and Dad had had enough of life without Betty.

Soon after Mum died, I'd changed my name for the final time. Born Marie Lawrie, I had become Lulu, then Mrs Gibb and Mrs Frieda. I now chose the name Lulu Kennedy-Cairns, wanting to combine a surname from my past – in this case my mother's birth family – with the name I'd been given and grown into. For me, it was about acknowledging every stage of my life because while my parents were complex, and had certainly made mistakes, our love as a family ran deep. I missed them both dreadfully.

# 64

# Down ... and Up Again

After the highs of 'Independence' and 'Relight My Fire', I think some part of me hoped that if things didn't carry on at the same level, they might at least not stall again. But, once again, I was at the mercy of a record industry that was constantly morphing, bigger labels swallowing up smaller ones, changes of personnel and strategy which often left music on the shelves and artists like me adrift.

It all started because I wanted to put out a new album featuring 'Where the Poor Boys Dance' plus all the other songs Billy and I had been writing. Despite being advised to carry on in the dance vein after the success of 'Independence', I knew I didn't want to get boxed in to one style and decided to ask Elton to listen to some of the material Billy and I had been working on because he's nothing if not brutally honest. He'd tell me if I stood any chance of getting another deal. But, after listening, Elton caught me off guard when he said he'd arrange a meeting with Rocket Records because he liked what we'd done.

I'd recorded with the label years before, but Elton's confidence this time around strengthened my own about the direction Billy and I were headed. We signed with Rocket and flew back to America to start work with a writer and producer called Dave Tyson, who'd co-written the hit 'Black Velvet'. And for the next eighteen months, we worked pretty much non-stop on the new album as I poured myself into it, which felt liberating one minute, gruelling the next. When the album was done, Elton called me from Japan to say he loved the material and I really felt it was work to be proud of. Every track said something, I'd co-written most of them and the result was an intensely personal album.

Then the record industry got in the way.

It was the late Nineties. The physical distribution of albums was still key and, as we started talking about releasing the *Poor Boys* album, the company doing Rocket's distribution was involved in a huge deal somewhere far up the chain which meant personnel changes and hold ups. When they told us they were delaying the album release for a year, I knew it was bad news. Albums are creative projects that need momentum, and shelving them destroys it. Amid all the change, it was clear that either the *Poor Boys* album had got forgotten or someone, some-where didn't believe in it. We were at the mercy of whoever was assigning budget, promotion and resources. And my new album wasn't getting any. Years later, we found out why. Someone we knew had been in the pub with some of the distribution execs around the time the *Poor Boys* album was completed.

'I've got to work on that fucking Lulu record,' one of them was heard to say.

I didn't know at the time that this was happening. But it makes sense now. The exec clearly had newer, shinier artists he wanted to work with and a record by someone who'd been around for years didn't figure in his plans. Maybe the fact that I was a middle-aged woman also didn't help. Plus, the music business is addicted to the now and the next, so unless you're a huge legacy artist, or someone really believes in your work, it's easy to get filed under 'has-been'.

A couple of tracks from the album eventually got released and the 'Where the Poor Boys Dance' single got to number twenty-four in early 2000. But I knew it wouldn't be enough to get more resources behind an album release. No one was really pushing the project and, at a time when people were still buying physical records, a hit wasn't created by the artist alone but a team who believed in it, promoted it and got it into shops. A TV show I'd agreed to do in the hope of keeping my profile up and getting someone at the label to notice had tanked as well.

Grieving my parents and with another record languishing at the bottom of someone's pile somewhere, it felt like I was – yet again – on a downward run on the roller coaster. But I'd been there before. I knew what I needed to do. And while I've been asked again and again over the years how I've managed to keep going so long, the answer is simple: I might fall over, or get pushed, but I don't stay down. I keep going because I always feel there's more to do. And I did the same then.

Billy and I kept writing and he started working with a young producer called Lukas Burton on a track called 'Inside Thing' which sampled 'Let 'Em In'. Written by Paul McCartney, it had been a hit for Wings and, although Billy and Lukas wanted me to send it to Paul, I wouldn't agree until we were sure it was worth his time. When we finally had something that felt right, I sent it and waited to hear back. If he didn't like it then no more would be said. I'd never want him to feel as if I was asking for a favour. But Paul soon wrote back saying it was 'fabulous' and asked a question that made us all gasp.

'Let me know how you want to proceed,' Paul wrote, still as approachable as he had been when I was a teenager.

I asked Paul if he'd record the track with me, he agreed and we booked studio time. Billy could hardly believe he was talking to McCartney from the mixing booth and, soon, the collaboration had sparked a new idea. Surely I could do more duets with old friends?

It was one of those times when everything feels as if it's flowing effortlessly. Elton suggested I get in touch with Louis Walsh, who'd had huge success managing acts including Boyzone and Westlife, and ask him to manage me. Louis kindly agreed. Then Colin Barlow, a great A&R man, got behind the idea. Belief in the project was building. Tom Jones had had a hit with *Reload* so now we just needed to decide who I was going to work with, songs, dates and locations. And, to do all that, we'd need to go through record companies, A&R men, managers and agents. What could possibly go wrong?

# 65

# The Stars Align

Sting and his wife Trudie Styler looked as if their limbs were made of rubber. I'd done a lot of yoga, but these two were next level. On the mat beside me, Jools Holland was just trying to get one leg crossed over the other as we tried to stifle our giggles. I jerked my head towards the door before we cat crawled out of the silent room.

I was at Sting and Trudie's country pile in Tuscany to record because Sting had agreed to sing with me for the duets album. And while fame and money don't always translate to taste, they certainly did for these two. The whole place – house, gardens, vineyard, food – was so magnificent, it felt like a dreamscape. One morning, I'd come out of my room to hear beautiful classical guitar music floating upwards from what I presumed were speakers. Walking down the sweeping stone staircase, I found Sting at the bottom, casually playing, one tanned leg up as he sat on a high-backed antique chair, like some kind of very chic travelling bard. If only every breakfast started that way.

We used the recording studio at the house to lay down the Beach Boys' 'Sail On, Sailor' and I also went to New York to record 'Now That the Magic Has Gone' with Joe Cocker. After going into the studio with him on 10 September 2001, I got on a flight back to London the following day, only for the plane to sit on the tarmac. Then the pilot announced there had been an incident in the centre of New York.

'If you look to the right of the plane, you will be able to see one of the Twin Towers burning,' he said to the shocked passengers.

Unimaginable. The city I'd always loved had suffered a devastating attack and so many innocent lives had been lost. Back in the terminal, I watched in horror with other passengers as the second tower collapsed. Like so many people, I will never forget that day. Somehow, Gail Federici and her husband Jimmy, who I'd been very close friends with for all the years since she'd worked with John, managed to get through all the roadblocks to reach me at the airport, and I spent the next five days with them, amid the grief, confusion and sadness.

Getting back to the UK, I felt drained but also determined to keep working on the album. A couple of the tracks were duets I'd already done: 'I'm Back for More' with Bobby Womack and 'Relight My Fire', of course. Elton, who was also exec producing the album, did 'Teardrops' with me and Cliff Richard, Marti Pellow and Russell Watson also agreed to sing. Plus, I duetted with newer acts who were flying at the time like Atomic Kitten, Westlife and Ronan Keating.

I was grateful to be working with such wonderful people and hoped in part it was down to the relationships I'd always tried to build and the reputation I'd made sure was 'grafter, dependable, always delivers' rather than 'diva, demanding, pain in the arse'. I'd learned early on just how unpredictable the business was, and knew it paid to treat everyone with respect because you never knew when you'd need a friend. Plus, there's no denying having Paul McCartney on the album was huge. How many musicians are going to say no to appearing on the same track listing as a Beatle? Paul had been there at the start of my career, and was helping me again now. I'll be forever grateful for his kindness.

Once again, I could sense buzz building around the album in the industry because there were so many great people involved. But everything went up another gear when I got a call from Lucian Grainge, the CEO and chairman of Universal, the man at the very top of the music business. Otherwise known as God.

'I'm excited about this album,' Lucian told me. 'It's going to be huge.'

With Lucian behind the project, I knew everything possible would be thrown at the album, particularly the marketing and promotion, and talks soon began about me doing *An Audience with . . .* Musicians including Elton, Tom Jones and Rod Stewart, as well as comedians like Dudley Moore, Barry Humphries and Victoria Wood, had all performed on the ITV show in front of a celebrity audience and, in the era of event terrestrial TV that everyone sat down together to watch, *An Audience with . . .* was a must-see. The show would go out to coincide with the album launch. And for the first time in a while, it felt as if the stars were really aligning again.

# 66

# Who Knew?

It took me years to stop thinking of calling Mum. I'd reach for my phone automatically before my brain caught up and I realised she wasn't there anymore. Losing her meant losing so many tiny everyday details – including the one person I always called if I wanted 'permission' to buy something.

'Oh, go on, treat yourself,' Betty would always say. 'You work so hard you deserve it hen.'

Staring at myself in the changing room mirror, I knew there was no way I should buy the leather jacket I'd just tried on. I had so many already. I didn't need another.

Did I?

I twisted the price tag to find out how much this one was.

I definitely didn't need it.

But then again, I had a big gig coming up and this fitted me like a glove. Butter-soft red leather, with fringing along the sleeves and an open back with lacing, it looked like a second skin. Incredible. I reached into my handbag and pulled out my mobile.

'I'm in Milan,' I said. 'In the Versace store. And I've tried on this jacket. It's spectacular. But, the thing is, I don't really need it.'

I'd rung the one person in the world I knew would encourage me just as enthusiastically as Betty ever had.

'Get it,' Elton said.

I love shopping, but I've never known anyone who can do it as passionately as he can.

I wore the jacket to perform 'River Deep, Mountain High' with Elton at the Rock for the Rainforest Concert at Carnegie Hall just a few weeks before the release of the duets album. Sting, who had founded the Rainforest Foundation Fund with Trudie, also sang, of course, and so did James Taylor. But the highlight for me was seeing the tenderness between Patti LaBelle and Nina Simone, who was in a wheelchair by then. Patti had accompanied Nina onto stage and it touched me deeply to see how gentle and respectful she was with her. None of us knew it would be one of Nina's last public performances, but she was as dignified and commanding as ever as she performed 'Here Comes the Sun', her drive to connect still burning out of her.

I returned home excited to film *An Audience with ...* which had finally been green-lit. The new album was called *Together* and I was going to sing with some of the artists I'd duetted with for the show, including Sting and Elton, as well as other special guests like Enrique Iglesias. But there was one person in particular who was arguably extra special. My director had suggested I ask Maurice to appear on the show, but while there was no bad blood between us anymore, it had been years since we'd last spoken.

'When and where?' Maurice said immediately when I called him at his home in Miami.

Always generous. Always kind. Maurice flew over and we performed the Bee Gees' 'First of May' – him at a piano, me standing beside, just as we'd done all those years ago as kids. I treasure the memory because Maurice died less than a year later at just fifty-three. It was such a huge, and premature, loss – not just of a talent who had so much left to give, but also of a man who was very loved.

Three days after *An Audience with* . . . was broadcast, *Together* was released in May 2002 and went straight to number four. I'd gone gold and the album's success was a huge moment for me. Just like always, I leaped on the upward wave, ready to speed with it for as long as possible, which was all-consuming. Not long after, for instance, I ended up sitting next to the film director Mike Figgis at a dinner. He told me he was making a documentary about the influence of the blues on Sixties British music and said he'd like me to be in it. I quickly agreed, knowing what a debt I owed those American greats who'd inspired me as a kid. The only problem was that I must have drunk so much that night I forgot what we'd agreed and almost dropped the phone when I got a call a few weeks later asking if I was set for the next day's filming.

'It's tomorrow?' I said, silently panicking.

Ever since my vocal problems, I'd made a point of restricting how much I talked for about a week before performing. But having forgotten all about Mike's project, I'd been going nineteen to the dozen as usual. I'd just have to do what I could and turned up at Abbey Road to find Jeff Beck on guitar and Jon Cleary on piano wating for me.

'We've just had Tom Jones in,' a voice said.

No pressure then.

We did 'Drown in My Own Tears' and Mike's film *Red, White and Blues* turned out to be one of a seven-part TV documentary series produced by Martin Scorsese on the history of the blues. Van Morrison, Tom, Eric and Stevie Winwood also appeared on the episode and, apart from some archival footage of Sister Rosetta Tharpe, I was the only woman who featured – although I'm pretty sure I wasn't the only woman back then who'd been inspired by the blues. Still, it felt good, as ever, to be in the company of contemporaries I so admired.

The next few years after *Together* felt like I had found a real rhythm at last. I did my first tour in a while and co-wrote another album – *Back on Track* – which was released in 2004, performed with Elton on his Peachtree Road Tour the following year, worked with Jools Holland, and did some dates with Take That on their Ultimate Tour in 2006. I was working with great friends, writing and recording material I loved and also reconnecting with my past in a good way. I was lucky enough for instance to appear on *American Idol*, after being invited to be a mentor in 2007 by my old friend Nigel Lythgoe. I performed a new arrangement of 'To Sir, With Love' by Barry Manilow, which gave the song an amazing new lease of life.

My work life was good. I had taken control of it at last. I was doing music I loved. But I was still only seeing half the story. There was more to life than work and, soon, other – far more personal – clouds began to gather on the horizon.

# IX

# 67

# What's Your Secret?

I walked over to the fridge, pulled out a bottle of wine and poured myself a large glass as I looked at the magazine cover. Emblazoned on the front, a picture of me, freeze-framed in a jump, hair flying and a huge smile across my face. Now I'd turned sixty, it felt as if all people ever wanted to talk about was how I looked.

'Can you tell me a bit about your beauty routine?'

'What's your secret?'

'Have you had any work done?'

I took a gulp of wine and stared at the picture. There were moments now when I hardly recognised myself. So much had happened, so much loss and change. And yet, still, here I was, smiling for the camera, answering all the questions, playing the role of 'Lulu'. I'd been doing it since I was a teenager, but after being in the business for almost forty years, seeing so much change, constantly reinventing and trying new things, it felt like most interviews were as superficial as the ones I'd done as a kid. I understood. People were interested. That's what sold. But the worst bit was that I really only had myself to blame for a lot of it.

I kept doing the interviews, for a start. Marian had drilled into me from the beginning that publicity was key. I was, as ever, trying to stay present and wanted to keep the upward curve going because a career like mine was dependent in part on public awareness of what I was doing. By and large, I'd always been treated very fairly by the press, and I was grateful for that, but, more and more, the articles felt like a caricature of a person rather than who I really was. That meant headlines about boys and fashion in my teens and twenties, motherhood in my thirties and forties, and men, menopause and ageing from about fifty onwards.

The men thing was simple: I'd had a few boyfriends, some great times, but wasn't interested in remarrying. I knew by now that I'd never want to live permanently with anyone again and, in many ways, enjoyed my independence in a way I'd have found impossible to believe when I was young. As far as ageing, I'd certainly done a bit to keep myself looking my best: some Botox and filler around my jaw, plus some kind of eye lift, although I honestly can't remember exactly what it was because it was so long ago. For me, my image was part of my work in the same way that athletes train their bodies.

But the constant interest in how I looked now also began to feel odd. I'd never been the most beautiful one, the thinnest one or the coolest one when I was young. I'd always been so insecure about my looks and had to work at it: clothes, make-up, hair. I'd learned a lot about how to make the most of myself along the way. But, increasingly now, it felt like every article was either about my 'big comeback' – for that, think everything I'd done from about the turn of the millennium because headline writers didn't seem to understand I was consistently working – plus how I managed to look so 'young'.

And then I'd made a decision which had seemed right at the time, but had only intensified the pressure.

'This is ridiculous,' Gail had said to me one day. 'We should do something about it. People are so interested we should tell them what you use.'

Gail and I had worked on projects together while she was still in business with John, and after the sale of their company too. So, given her experience, it felt like an obvious step to launch a beauty line together. I've never been on the breadline, but certainly didn't have enough money to give up and sit on a desert island for the rest of my life because I'd signed deals years before that were very different to the ones artists have today.

Put it all together and developing my own beauty products for a range called Time Bomb had seemed like a good business idea. Gail and I started working with her chemist Joe Cincotta to create affordable formulas based on cutting-edge ingredients, launched the brand and it had felt empowering at first to go into business in my late fifties. I enjoyed developing the products, as well as being the 'face' of the brand and promoting it. But while Time Bomb did very well for a few years, Gail and I both knew it would take a lot of work to grow it into something even bigger. By then, she'd started Color Wow, another hair line, which was taking up a lot of her time and I had my career too. So my work with Time Bomb eventually reached a natural end.

But running a beauty line also inevitably means you end up thinking even more about your appearance and, somehow during those years, it all got gradually wrapped into much bigger questions about ageing. Part of it was inevitable. I don't think many people get to midlife without asking some questions about where they've been and where they'll end up. And, for women in particular, losing your role as a carer is hard. It's who we are for so many years of our lives, after all. And perhaps I found it particularly hard because I'd been looking after people since I was a child. I'd never stopped. It was who I was. And now there was no one who needed looking after anymore.

Increasingly now, thoughts about the past, and the future, preoccupied me. Why had I made some of the career choices I had? Had my life ever really been my own since I was a kid? What would the future look like for me? And just how long could I constantly morph, reinvent and bounce back in the music industry? Then again, who would I be if I didn't?

I had always kept going, tried to be upbeat, but now I felt alone in a way I never had before because although I was close to family and friends, I still came back to an empty home at the end of most days. And my mind, which had turned relentlessly ever since I was a child, raced more and more without the distraction of other people.

Looking back down at the magazine, I picked it up, dropped it into the bin and determined to stop feeling so sorry for myself. Then I walked back to the fridge, took out the bottle and filled up my glass again.

# 68

# Three Is My Favourite Number

The powerhouse that is Anastacia was nothing if not straight-talking. It was the first day of rehearsals for a UK tour I was doing with her and Chaka Khan. And it seemed like something our dancers, who had been choreographed by Gareth Walker, had done hadn't gone down well with Anastacia.

'This is going to be hard work,' Gail's husband Jimmy said to me.

He wasn't wrong. Together, the three of us had collectively survived the music industry for five decades and weren't afraid to speak our minds. And if I was a live wire then so were Anastacia and Chaka Khan. All of us were used to performing solo and between trying to stand my ground and deploy every weapon in my arsenal of tact and diplomacy, I got so stressed I lost my voice. But by the time we'd finished rehearsals, the three of us had gelled, were bouncing off each other on stage and had an absolute blast when we did the Here Come the Girls tour in 2009. The following year, Anastacia and I went out on the road again for a second leg of the tour, this time with Heather Small.

Rehearsals and planning, performing and hotel rooms, late nights trying to bring myself down from the high of performing with a few glasses of wine, but knowing I had to get up again in the morning and move on to the next venue. And, in between it all, my thoughts which turned ever inward, keeping work going while feeling like I was no longer propelling forwards in the way I always had, and feeling increasingly anxious.

And it was then, somehow, somewhere, that I made a fatal mistake. I stopped being vigilant. I no longer took care. Almost twenty years after leaving The Meadows, I'd talked about my childhood and divorce, attended group meetings for the children of alcoholics, meditated and studied. I thought I'd done everything I needed to.

But remember the guy and the elephants? The point where you think you've got it all under control is one of the most dangerous places to be. Because this is precisely the moment you stop watching so closely and things slowly start to slip out of control. Or at least they did for me. And the worst part was that I'd had so much practice at performing, I was able to completely hide what was happening from everyone.

But even as I kept playing my part perfectly professionally, just as I'd always done, my life started to spin downwards in private.

# 69

# Into the Deep

Very quietly, and very secretly, my drinking was slowly spiralling out of control. Bit by bit, night by night, it slipped from something I'd always done to relax, be social and fun, to a compulsion. Exactly when it got out of control, I can't tell you, but that's the thing about alcoholism: it can creep up on you so quietly, you're almost unaware. Alcohol is such a socially acceptable drug after all; everyone is doing it, and you're just joining in the party right? Have another glass of Chardonnay. You're not doing cocaine night after night. You're knocking off the edges and who doesn't do that? But this is exactly what makes the boundary between social drinking and addiction so hard to pinpoint. And also why I was able to ignore the problem for a really long time.

The technical term for this is denial.

One small word for such a powerful emotional tool. Denial doesn't mean I didn't know I had a problem. On some level, I absolutely knew I did. I'd always been afraid that I might one day, given my family history. But denial allowed me to ignore the truth and, instead of seeing I had an addiction, I blamed the easiest target: myself. The drink wasn't the problem – I was.

I was a master at this kind of misdirection, of course. I'd been steeped in it as a child and honed it to perfection as a teenage performer: keep smiling, don't let anyone in, stay hidden. So, even as my drinking slid out of hand, I kept it completely secret and no one had a clue what was happening – not my friends, my child or my family, and certainly not my work colleagues. I never drank until I finished work and, on days off, I would start drinking at around 5pm, more often than not out with friends or at an event, and was careful to keep pace with what everyone else was having. I also wouldn't touch a drop in situations when I knew drinking could be dangerous, like an evening when I babysat my grandchildren. But then I'd get home, the dark thoughts would crowd in and I'd carry on. And on. I drank secretly, alone. And even as it felt like my life was slipping away from me, the contortions of my denial were endless. I thought I was controlling alcohol, but in reality it was controlling me.

I won't drink tonight.

Just one.

I'll wait until the weekend.

I'll cut back.

I'll have an early night.

I haven't got a problem.

But I could never stick to the many bargains I made with myself and, as the drinking hours slipped late into the night, it created a web of feelings I needed more and more alcohol to numb. Guilt, embarrassment and, most of all, shame. I wasn't a young girl who didn't know any better. I was in my sixties. How had I let this happen? What kind of person was I?

The shame that filled me is indescribable.

I was an embarrassment. Two marriages. A career that had gone up and down. I'd let down my son. I'd done the meditation and therapy and was still a mess. What was wrong with me? Why couldn't I stop? Where was my life going to end up? Could I keep my career going as I got older? Who would be interested in an old drunk? And underneath it all was the worst kind of guilt: I was my father's daughter.

But the real kicker? The more you drink, the worse you feel, and the more you drink to numb the pain. And so it goes on. Because addiction is dependent on the false myths it creates, whispering that all you need is another hit to forget the secrets it has 'revealed'. And mine were that I was just not good enough and the only way I could be loved was by pretending to be someone else because if you really did see me, you wouldn't like me. The shame and confusion of my childhood had rooted such powerful beliefs so deeply inside me that nothing – love, music, friends or family – could erase them. I had outrun them for years. Always looking to please people and be loved. Always on. Always delivering. Trying to keep everyone safe and happy. But the weight of my constant movement had finally caught up with me. And the thought of admitting my addiction terrified me because I thought other people would also realise at last that I wasn't enough. So I spiralled ever downwards. Anything to avoid having to admit what was happening.

The truth is I am an alcoholic. The child of an alcoholic. The grandchild of an alcoholic. And it's taken me years to get to the point where I'm finally prepared to admit it in the public domain.

But now I am.

# 70

# Strictly Incompatible

E very alcoholic is different, but, for me, it meant life ended up polarised between two very distinct points: the ridiculous and the sublime. And *Strictly Come Dancing* definitely wasn't sublime.

It would be easy to blame everything on alcohol, but, once again, I carefully managed my drinking and always kept it very separate from work. I turned up and delivered throughout the years when I was drinking because I was as disciplined about my addiction as I was about my work. But the alcohol certainly affected my emotional landscape. I was privately weaker and more sensitive than usual, which is probably why doing the show hit me so hard.

Brendan Cole and I didn't like each other from the off. He was a foot taller than me for a start and I didn't understand why I'd been paired with someone so tall. But his manner was also difficult. The first thing he did when we got paired in front of the cameras was fling me over his shoulder, which everyone laughed at. Myself included. I even went so far as to say I was 'thrilled' in an interview. But, deep down, it felt like a power move. Aged sixty-two, I didn't know whether to laugh or cry.

So, it wasn't the easiest start to our relationship and things just got worse when I couldn't perform how either of us wanted me to. I'd expected to enjoy the learning process, thought it would be joyful and fun, because I'd always been willing to push myself into new areas and learn new skills. This time, though, I just felt tense. I'm no pushover and understood Brendan wanted to do well, as did I, but a bit more carrot and less stick would have worked better from my teacher.

'I think I'm a very nice person,' Brendan said in an interview on the show. 'Most people I work with, I get along with. Most. Watch this space.'

I loved all the other contestants on the show, but being stuck in a room with Brendan for hours every day felt pretty gruelling. He's since called me 'difficult'. I'd say he wasn't a very clever psychologist because there are ways to get the best out of your student.

There are always three sides to a story – yours, mine and the truth – and I don't think Brendan enjoyed the experience much either. I meanwhile would go home at the end of the working week and wonder if I could just somehow drop out. I couldn't, of course. It's not my style. I never quit. But then another working week in the dance studio would start and it was increasingly clear that, while I could move and had timing, I just wasn't a very good technical ballroom dancer, so I tried to find ways to get round the problem. Early on, for instance, I thought it might be a good idea to make me the butt of the joke by doing more comedy in the routines. A message came one manager to another that I shouldn't be trying to advise Brendan on what to do.

Then I bought him a bloody expensive Japanese lunch in an attempt to relax over some food and form a friendship. My charms didn't work on him. Nothing seemed to stick.

The tenser I got, the worse I did and it felt very difficult to 'fail' so publicly. I was hardest on myself, of course, and blamed everything on my failings, replaying the old script of 'not delivering'. The relief I felt when I got voted off in week six was intense. It felt like I'd been let out of jail.

A very popular myth about addicts is that you can spot them because their lives have clearly fallen apart, but it's not true. There are many people who, like me, function as 'normal': work, keep their life together and completely mask their private behaviour. That's how I could keep going on *Strictly*, and also rise to challenges like the night I performed at B. B. King's Blues Club & Grill in New York. It was a huge moment for me to be in the place that he had created and perform on a stage where greats including James Brown, Ray Charles and Etta James had sung. I didn't carry so much baggage with me in America, and knew a lot of people in the audience had probably not seen me since 'To Sir, With Love', so I didn't go onto the stage with a back catalogue of songs I 'had' to perform. I just stood there as a musician, chose music I loved and sang it with the wonderful Fab Faux band led by the equally wonderful Paul Shaffer.

It was a magical night.

But whether it's a high, or a low, you still go home alone at the end of the night. They say you're only as sick as your secrets and, as the years passed, I was afraid that mine were slowly killing me.

# 71

# Rock Bottom

It was 3 November 2013, the day of my sixty-fifth birthday, and I'd just cooked lunch for family and friends. A happy occasion. A celebration of a milestone. We'd crowded around my long dining table, eaten, chatted and I'd smiled through it, all the while knowing that, night after night now, I found myself curled on the floor, sobbing and praying to God to give me the strength to stop myself drinking as the weight of my addiction grew ever heavier.

I was so tired of it. The hiding, the shame.

As people drifted away, I sat at the dining table, listening, but also ever so slightly withdrawn, as I was so often these days, as Edwina and her daughter Azalea chatted.

'I think he's just holding on by his fingernails,' my niece said as she spoke about a man she knew who was having problems.

And, almost without thinking, the words tumbled out of me.

'He's not the only one,' I said softly.

Edwina looked at me steadily.

'I know,' she said. 'And I've known for quite some time.'

I stared at her in disbelief. Edwina knew? But she'd never said a thing. All my siblings, however, had struggled in their own ways and, eventually, started to see what was happening with me. But they also knew I had to be the one to ask for help. Edwina reached out and took my hand as I stared at her aware that, underneath the weight I'd been feeling for so long, was a new feeling. Relief. Like a gasp of air as you come up from underneath the water.

'I think I need to go into rehab, don't you?' I said.

Edwina nodded.

Twenty-four hours later I arrived at Heathrow to catch a plane back to The Meadows for six weeks of treatment. Never underestimate the courage it takes for anyone to admit an addiction. But what I learned that day with my sister is that if you can't be vulnerable enough to admit what's happening, people can't reach far in enough to help. One short conversation had opened the door for me to start my recovery. Edwina didn't question me or ask for a long conversation. She just helped me plan, pack and prepare, which was exactly what I needed.

The boarding call for my flight was echoing around the departure lounge as I pulled my mobile out of my bag and made a call.

'Jordan?' I said.

'Hi Mum. Are you okay? I'm pretty busy. Can I call back later?'

'No darling. I'm just getting on a flight.'

'Where to?' Jordan asked, surprised. 'You didn't tell me you were going away.'

I took a deep breath.

'I'm going to America. To rehab.'

There was a pause before Jordan finally spoke. He sounded confused. I knew he would be. He, like so many others, had no idea.

'Wait a minute, wait a minute,' he said. 'Rehab for what Mum?'

'I'm an alcoholic.'

Another pause.

'What?' Jordan exclaimed. 'Are you sure?'

'Yes. I've been sure for a while.'

I felt as if I was standing on a precipice, waiting for my son to realise exactly what kind of mother he had.

'I love you Mum,' Jordan finally said. 'And I'm proud of you. I'm here for you.'

# 72

# Recovery

Here are two key facts I learned over the next six weeks at The Meadows.

'You've had complex post-traumatic stress disorder since you were a child because you lived in a war zone,' a therapist told me gently as I resisted the idea that this was the reason for years of sleep difficulties, anxiety and continual running to try to stop myself from falling down.

It was like learning a completely new language as I was taught about the effects of childhood trauma and the complex dance it creates between feelings that are completely shut down, while also creating a constant emotional storm. The second fact was that addiction is an illness which ran in my family, just as heart disease or cancer does in others. The idea that I was ill, rather than just weak, a failure or a bad person, was very powerful for me.

The biggest part of recovery, however, isn't factual, it's emotional. And, at times, very painful. In the weeks that followed, sitting in rooms with people who were also addicted to anything from drugs to food and talking our way into the most private and personal corners of our lives, I had to wrestle with guilt, shame and everything in between as I finally accepted that I had never really been truly open with anyone. Fear had been so fused inside me as a child that it had made me terrified of everything – sex, drugs, but, most of all, being seen. I'd submersed myself in my parents' battles and was primed to do whatever anyone asked of me in the pursuit of approval and love from the moment I started working. However much it had cost me, though, I'd never wanted to complain. Instead, I'd told myself how lucky I was.

But how can you build a sense of self on the mirage of 'fame'?

It isn't real. And because no one had been able to give me any rules and regulations to navigate the experience, I'd just made them up for myself and carried all the fear from my childhood into an adult life structured around the intricate defence mechanisms I'd built to keep myself safe.

Packing up everything from my childhood and locking it away had served me well in many ways. I'd been able to delay the inevitable for years through distraction, focusing on the next project and throwing on new identities and personas. The difference between me and my father however was that I hid my addiction. I'd paid a heavy price for refusing to go deep enough to access my most difficult feelings about my childhood. It was clear I needed to do more work to feel – and process – the pain. And while the breakdown of my marriage to John had certainly forced some of it out into the open with the realisation that I had lost myself in other people and relationships, I still hadn't connected to what lay beneath the relentless need for love and approval.

It was the shame of a child living amid violence and addiction which still lay deep inside me like sediment at the bottom of a lake; the belief that I had to be perfect in order to be loved and the need for control those feelings had created, as well as the drive to be responsible for others to avoid ever having to focus on myself. And also, the impact of becoming famous so young had made me bury those feelings even deeper, believing I had to perform constantly to please everyone and keep striving.

That is where I needed to go to trace the roots of my addiction.

Rehab allowed me to start seeing clearly and finally free myself of the weight of my need to be perfect in order to get approval. I'd sensed years before that focusing on spirituality would be vital for me and knew now that I had to focus more deeply on my spiritual practice as I continued to examine not only how my choices had impacted me, but also others. I wasn't just a victim of my past. I'd made many mistakes. But now I realised I didn't need to be 'cured', 'fixed' or Little Miss Perfect. I wasn't broken, just human. And I started to realise that, instead of being whoever I believed people wanted me to be, I had to give myself permission to just be. Myself. Just as I was. I finally started to learn to let go.

Most of all, I learned that believing you can manage addiction on your own is both the ultimate form of ego, but also self-harm. We all need help. I'd blamed and shamed myself for years. Now, I had to sit, listen and be open to seeing the world in all its complex, painful, but joyful, shades. It was the child in me who saw things in black and white, good and bad. Now, as an adult, I finally started to learn that it's possible to feel very different emotions all at once without betraying yourself or others. I could be honest about the positives and negatives, and forgive my own failings, as well as those of my parents. They were just two broken kids who recognised something in each other and had tried to do their best for us while also carrying their own scars.

Recovery is day by day. And that never stops. But I knew as I left America that I couldn't waste the precious chance I'd been given.

# 73

# Now I Know What to Do

Two years on from leaving The Meadows, I released my most personal album ever. Coming out of rehab and back into normal life is complex, but you just have to put what you've learned into practice, day by day. And I'd also come to realise that alcoholism had been a blessing in many ways: it had forced a reckoning inside myself that I'd needed for years. Now, I was completely committed to my recovery and thankful that I was still as clear as I had been on the day I left The Meadows, aware and using all the tools at my disposal: meetings, meditation and study.

The new album was called *Making Life Rhyme* and it was a return to my rock roots. It would probably have been easier, and a lot more financially dependable, to take up offers of touring with other singers from the Sixties. But I had always wanted to move forwards and not get stuck in the past. And after going back to where it had all started and signing again to Decca, I still wanted to evolve. If 'Shout' had expressed emotions I didn't even know I had, the tracks on *Making Life Rhyme* addressed feelings about my alcoholism, recovery and spiritual practices.

I wasn't ready to put it all out there yet and didn't want headlines about addiction to scream above the music. But I did write explicitly about my experiences and have wondered ever since if anyone listening connected to the truths in them. I hope so.

'Poison Kiss', for instance, captures my experiences of alcoholism:

Well I guess my resistance was low
The way you crept up on me slow
For years I always said no
But you always knew that I would follow you
Cos you're not a friend … you're a sin
And when your addiction kicks in
There is no way your victim can win
Cause you break em inside and every promise lies
It's your poison kiss
I just can't resist
It was your poison kiss
Got me addicted to you

While 'Every Single Day' is about recovery:

Things started slipping
When I started seeing you on my own
You were my little secret
But I couldn't keep a secret for long
It's the same ol' story
You heard it all before

No-one's gonna worry
'til you're lying on the floor
How much will it take?
'til you find out you can't take it no more?
No more, baby.
Every single day I'm living like the last
Every single day I'm changing so fast
Things are better every single day
Now I know what to do

I'd known music was healing since childhood, and the creation of *Making Life Rhyme* was very much about that. The lyrics of 'Every Single Day' summed up the sense of freedom I felt after getting back to London, attending meetings and reconnecting to my spiritual path, as well as using the new tools I'd learned in recovery. I meditated every day, read, wrote and was feeling the joy as well as the pain because you can't have one without the other. It's called being human. And I also knew now that there was always a solution, even if I had to look to find it.

Billy and I had a ball writing and recording *Making Life Rhyme*. We did it on a shoestring with musicians we admired and I felt like I'd come home to the people and music that had always rooted me. The album did okay, it charted, and most of the critics loved the work. But the greatest gift now was simply the act of creating music that finally felt truly honest.

Death and rebirth. I'd had so many. But this was the most precious one.

# 74

# Kate Moss and La Croisette

B etween shivering on the bank of the Thames freezing my arse off after going into the river that Kate Moss had 'disappeared' in to drive a key plot point, and standing under a bright blue Côte d'Azur sky watching Jennifer Saunders and Joanna Lumley sink very slowly into a swimming pool while sitting in a tiny three-wheeled French delivery van, being part of the *Ab Fab* movie was a riot.

Jennifer had assembled such a star-studded cast, I didn't know which direction to look in. Filming had kicked off with a party scene featuring everyone from Jon Hamm, who was almost as beautiful as Rock Hudson, to Jerry Hall. But when Eddie accidentally knocked Kate off a balcony during the party – and into the Thames – I also had to fall in for some reason. All I know is that I spent an entire day wet, the scene got cut and that's movie-making.

Luckily, there was more sunshine when we flew to the south of France, where Eddie and Patsy had fled to escape criminal charges over Kate's disappearance. In a rage with my ever-unreliable PR Eddie, I decided to follow and confront her. When filming wrapped late one evening, Jennifer, June

Whitfield, Julia Sawalha, Jane Horrocks and I ended up going out for dinner and walking back along the Croisette singing at the tops of our voices together. It felt like the end of an era. You never know, though. I hope not.

But as one year in recovery turned into two, three and more, I had been given the gift of knitting together a life that felt hopeful, both professionally and personally. Contentment, peace, connection – those are ideas I believe in, and I had at last started to build my life on these solid pillars. I'd never felt better, in fact. They call it the pink cloud. And I was floating on it for years, enjoying myself, free of all the old negative voices.

I was performing again, doing some acting in things like *Ab Fab* and, later, a film called *Arthur's Whisky* with Diane Keaton and Patricia Hodge. I also went back on stage in 2018 to appear in *42nd Street* in the West End. The real stars of the show were the dancers, of course, but it felt like another full-circle moment because just as Jordan had once come to see me at the theatre, my grandchildren, Bella and Teddy, now came to visit between shows and we'd eat chips before trying out some tap dancing together. Brendan would have loved it. My grandchildren had always been joyful, but I could now connect to them more fully than ever before. And they have healed a sadness that stayed with me for years about not having more children.

Arguably, however, one of the most electric moments professionally of recent years was appearing with Take That again. Kim Gavin has always creatively directed their tours and each one is spectacular. But for 2019's Odyssey tour he gave me my most fabulous stage entrance ever – standing in a huge open half sphere set 100 feet above the stage.

'Are you sure?' Gary had exclaimed when Kim told us what he wanted to do.

'Let's try and we'll see,' Kim replied.

It was certainly high. But I felt like I was flying as I looked down on a crowd of thousands and belted out the opening lines of 'Relight My Fire' before the boys took over below me. All our lives had changed. Robbie and Jason were no longer with the band, while Gary, Mark and Howard were now dressed far more soberly than they ever had been in the Nineties. But being back with them felt possibly even more adrenaline-inducing than before. Racing down the stairs from the sphere to reach the wings of the stage, I'd wait for Gary to welcome me on each night with the same words.

'And here she is,' he'd roar. 'The Queen.'

When we'd first got together to prepare for the tour, I swear a look of relief had flashed over the boys' faces when they heard I could still hold the notes. Now, as I stood on stage with them, sober and clear, I allowed myself to soak in every moment with the men – and fans – who'd been in and out of my life so joyfully for so many years. I had had my share of downs, but the joy now shone more brightly than it ever had.

X

# 75

# Thank You for Leaving Me

I sat at the restaurant table looking at John. Almost fifty years on from first meeting, and twenty-five after our divorce, we'd become closer. John was now happily remarried and a father to two more children while I'd stayed single, but what had brought us together in the first place had reconnected us again, older and wiser: shared interests and a deep connection as both people, parents and grandparents.

It was 2022 and, like everyone else, we'd weathered the storm of Covid before coming blinking back out into life. I'd got it early on and had felt the effects linger for months afterwards. But I'd also kept busy as I isolated at home. I love my work, so, lockdown or no lockdown, I was going to carry on. I continued my acting classes on Zoom, wrote with Billy remotely and also realised I was going to be driven up the wall if I wore a tracksuit much longer, so I got in touch with friends and did some wonderful Instagram Lives with people like Tricky Stewart, David Furnish, Sir Tim Rice, Douglas Stuart, Alan Cumming, Fearne Cotton and David Lammy to name a few.

Getting my CBE during that strange time, though, was a far lonelier experience. I'd had a very nice chat with King – then

Prince – Charles when I got my OBE in 2000 at Buckingham Palace. I'd always admired him because he was so ahead of his time on things like food and architecture. But my CBE for services to music, entertainment and charity simply dropped through the letterbox and onto the front mat. Over twenty years on from losing my parents, I thought a lot about them that day, knowing how much it would have meant to them. Wee Marie had a CBE.

Now, as the world got finally – and fully – back to normal after the pandemic, I looked at John. There was a conversation we needed to have. One I'd been thinking about for a while. I'd been in recovery for several years now and, throughout it all, I had made sure I remained vigilant, carried on checking and balancing, trying to unravel the complex journey that is any life. And John had been, and still is, an important part of mine. We both say that we're now closer than ever.

'I need to thank you,' I said to him.

'What for?'

'For leaving.'

John looked at me. I knew he'd also reflected on the past and had carried a lot of sadness about how things had ended and my separation from Jordan.

'What do you mean?' he said.

'Just what I say. I'm grateful to you for what you did.'

'Why?'

'Because it was the start of a new beginning for me and forced me to address things. As painful as it was, you were a catalyst. We needed to separate because I needed to change.'

Sometimes, it takes years to unravel what happened and why, but I truly believe everything has a purpose. John has been one of the many teachers I've been lucky enough to have in my life. I've learned to be grateful for what I have, let go of resentment and forgive.

# 76

# One Lucky Girl

Gratitude filled me as I stood under the stage lights of the London Palladium. It was the end of a sold-out tour to mark sixty years in the music business, night after night standing on stage doing what I loved, still filled with as much energy and enthusiasm as I'd ever had.

I looked out into the audience before turning my head towards the wings where some special guests were waiting to join me.

'So you want to meet my family?' I said and the audience roared.

Six decades is a long time in the music industry and the idea to mark them with the 'Champagne for Lulu' tour had been sparked by sorting through old pictures. When you do something for long enough, you forget so much, and I've certainly been guilty of focusing on the dips and forgetting the highs. But, as I finally started to catalogue years of photographs, I thought deeply about just how far I'd come. Old black and whites of me with Robert Plant and Stevie Wonder. More recent pictures with Elton and Paul. Some of them hung on a wall in my home, pictures that traced my story and work with so many amazing artists in some wonderful places. My career has always been layered – not just in terms of different types of work, but also the many tones of joy, challenge, loss and success.

I'd had a great 2023 with some huge gigs – Hyde Park with Take That and the Hollywood Bowl with Culture Club. I also had a wonderful team around me now: my new managers Shoshanna Stone and Mark Strange, as well as Gail Federici, my constant sounding board for over forty years. We'd worked hard to create the true story of some of the defining moments of my life and, in between songs, I also spoke to audiences because that's the beauty of getting older isn't it? You can finally look back and begin to trace the shapes and patterns of your life that have come to define you. Some people think it's all down to coincidence, but I believe it's fate – all those moments that thread together to tell the story of who you are and how you came to be.

We also used film in the show because I wanted the audience to be able to see the journey as well as hear it, and shine a light on some of those who had most influenced me. We found wonderful footage of some of the artists I'd worked with and I sung with them again as they appeared on the screen behind me. Maurice and I 'performed' 'First of May' again, I did 'The Man Who Sold the World' with David Bowie, and duetted with Tina Turner on 'I Don't Wanna Fight'.

Eighteen dates. Eighteen nights of laughter – and some tears – as I looked back and thanked all those who'd supported me for so long. Because apart from my siblings, my longest relationship has always been with my audience. So many people have stuck with me through it all and this tour was my chance to thank them using the performance skills I'd honed over so many years.

Back in the Sixties, I'd acted on pure instinct. Now, I found a deep pleasure in being an older performer who knew how to take an audience with me on a deeper journey. Going home to Glasgow was particularly emotional. Gary, Mark and Howard had joined me on stage in Manchester and now my family were waiting to come on to the Palladium stage – sixty years to the day since the release of 'Shout'.

'Come and join me,' I called and they walked hesitantly out into the spotlights, squinting into the glare.

Jordan was there, of course, with my daughter-in-law Alanna, my grandchildren and John. But Billy, Edwina and Gordon too with their spouses and my nephews and nieces. Twenty-one of us in total. Three generations of the family Betty and Eddie had created – my brothers, sister and me all moving far beyond the circumstances we were born into and finally breaking the cycle to make sure our children's futures looked different.

'Teddy, Bella,' I said and beckoned for my grandson and granddaughter to come and join me.

Minutes before, I'd closed the show with the song I'd chosen to perform on every date because it so perfectly said what I needed it to: 'I'm Still Standing'. No truer words. Thanks Elton. Now, it was time for the encore and, as I looked at my musical director Rick Krieve. He got it.

And the song?

'Shout', of course.

With the two precious fixed points that have always sustained me – my family surrounding me and my audience out in front – I started to sing.

# Epilogue

A few months after the Palladium date, I arrived at Glastonbury in the summer of 2024 where blue skies shone above the fields of Worthy Farm. It was a hot, sunny day as I made my way through the crowds.

'Hey Lulu!' voices called as I walked towards the stage.

Meeting so many different generations is special when you've been around for as long as I have and I love that young people today still connect to 'Shout' in particular because of its timeless energy.

I was at Glastonbury to perform with my band and also my sister on backing vocals. Performing these days feels even more like coming home than it ever did. I've found musicians I trust completely and there's a shorthand between us that feels precious. The crowd roared as I walked onto the stage and soaked in every molecule of that special energy. I was home.

The deep connection I feel when I perform still reaches the same place inside it has done since I was a child. Because as much as I interact with an audience, it's also an internal process, joining up parts of myself to become fully whole. I've always loved my work, but the difference today is that I'm no longer a fearful child singing for love and to be seen, but a grown woman who has chosen joy and the connectedness I experience through my job. It's my happy place. Plus, I think everyone has a talent, but I was lucky to be able to identify mine early and my way of expressing that very primal force has always been through the music.

Connection and creativity: two key themes of my life. The other, of course, is my spiritual journey, developing and nourishing an inner life to allow me to better serve others through the music. It healed me as a child, united me to something beyond myself, and now I share that with others. This, I believe, is my purpose.

If I had one piece of advice for young artists today, it would be this: stay true to that inner drive and never sever the link to your authentic self by believing the hype around 'fame'. It's thrilling certainly, and can open up your world in ways you would never have dreamed of. But there are darker sides too – the crashes, insecurity, distrust and loss of self. Fame alone is not fulfilling, so beware of pursuing it for its own sake. Plus, I also believe it's partly about destiny. Failure is another key part of any career and, while it's taught me so much, I've seen many people crushed by the lows, or finding harmful ways of coping with the highs.

It was never the plan to travel as far as I did. I was just lucky to be able to channel something inside myself, be in the right place at the right time and get some breaks that propelled me forwards. But, ultimately, music has been the catalyst for my real learning. Life has many layers and each stage of my career allowed me to deal with them piece by piece. I'm not done yet. It's an ongoing process. All any of us can do is keep curious, keep learning and keep growing. Plus, cultivate humility and gratitude, even for the hard stuff.

I can honestly say now that I wouldn't change a single thing. Every setback and success, the highs and lows, have brought me to where I believe I'm meant to be. We draw people and events towards us, even the difficult ones, because we hopefully learn from the challenges so we don't repeat the same mistakes and ultimately become wiser. I feel more alive now than I ever have before. More present. More joyful. For now, there's more to learn, music to write, songs to sing and life to live. In fact, I feel as enthusiastic about these things today as I ever have and grateful for the grace that has pervaded my life.

And that's the most precious part of my whole story really. I spent decades never feeling worthy, hypervigilant, bending myself into shapes I knew deep down didn't fit, and often in my younger years being whoever people wanted me to be. But I have finally realised perhaps the most important thing. I started out as Marie, today I'm Lulu, and both are inside me. I'm more comfortable in my own skin now than I've ever been.

Not long ago, I was out walking my dog when a man stopped me in the street.

'You're Lulu aren't you?' he asked.

'I am,' I replied.

'You always look like you've having a good time when I see you on the telly,' he said brightly. 'Enjoying yourself. Living your best life.'

And he was right.

I thanked him, smiled one more time and we said goodbye as I turned to start walking down the street again.

Living my best life.

# Acknowledgements

Over the years, I've learned that everything works better when you're in a community. No woman is an island. Thanks to all of you who read, advised, jogged my memory and helped me reach back to bring everything into the open.

My incredible management team Shoshanna Stone and Mark Strange.

Peter Cross, for your endless counsel.

Megan Lloyd Davies, who brought me to life on the page.

My literary agent Oscar Janson-Smith.

Susannah Otter – plus the whole Hodder team – for your tremendous support and hard work.

Gail Federici, my hidden hand.

And to those of you who I haven't mentioned – you know who you are and my heartfelt appreciation to you all!

# Picture Acknowledgements

Page 1, above: courtesy of Billy Kennedy. Below: © Popperfoto via Getty Images/Getty Images.

Page 2, above: © ITV/Shutterstock. Below: © PictureLux/The Hollywood Archive/Alamy.com.

Page 3, above: © Koh Hasebe/Shinko Music/Getty Images. Below: © Rolls Press/Popperfoto via Getty Images/Getty Images.

Page 4, above: © P. Shirley/Daily Express/Hulton Archive/Getty Images. Below: © Mark and Colleen Hayward/Getty Images.

Page 5, above, left and below, right: © Ken McKay/Shutterstock.

Page 6, above: © Photoshot/TopFoto. Below: © Jordan Peck/Getty Images.

Page 7, above: © Fox Searchlight/Courtesy Everett Collection/Alamy.com. Below: © Andy Catlin/Alamy.com.

Page 8, above, left: courtesy of Lulu. Above, right: courtesy of Mark Strange. Below: © Samir Hussein/WireImage/Getty Images.